Vandevert

The Hundred Year History of a Central Oregon Ranch

By Ted Haynes and Grace Vandevert McNellis

The Robleda Company, Publishers / Menlo Park, CA

Publisher's Cataloging-in-Publication
(Provided by Quality Books, Inc.)

Haynes, Ted.

Vandevert : the hundred year history of a central Oregon ranch / by Ted Haynes and Grace Vandevert McNellis.

p. cm.

Includes bibliographical references and index.

LCCN 2010935162

ISBN-13: 978-0-9646506-2-6

ISBN-10: 0-9646506-2-2

1. Ranches--Oregon--Deschutes County--History--19th century. 2. Ranches--Oregon--Deschutes County--History --20th century. 3. Frontier and pioneer life--Oregon. 4. Deschutes County (Or.)--Biography. 5. Oregon--History, Local. I. McNellis, Grace Vandevert, 1929- II. Title.

F882.D4H39 2011 979.5'87

QBI10-600208

Cover and book design by Marin Bookworks
Printed in the United States of America

The Robleda Company, Publishers
1259 El Camino Real Ste. 2720
Menlo Park, CA 94025

650-323-3006

Inheriting the original owner's name along with a ranch was like being knighted, honored, passed the baton, entrusted with something precious. If their experience had ended badly you felt it your obligation to right it. If their experience had gone well, you felt an obligation to continue that legacy.

ELLEN WATERSTON

Table of Contents

Introduction

When Vandevert Ranch was founded in 1892, Central Oregon had one person for every three square miles of land. Deschutes County did not exist and neither did the city of Bend. As the area grew up around them, the Vandevert family contributed to its progress and remained among the best-known and highly respected members of the community. The ranch saw good times and bad, the privations of the Great Depression, the direct effects of two world wars, and the boom times of the 1910s, 1920s, and 1990s. Vandevert Ranch has existed for over a century: welcoming Indians, raising cattle, cutting timber, educating children, and adapting to the late arrival of modern civilization to what was—well into the 20th century—still a frontier.

Grace Vandevert McNellis has been collecting memoirs, photographs, articles, and title records from all over Oregon for more than 30 years. Yet the richest source for the history of the ranch remains Grace's memory. Grace was born on the ranch and grew up there in the 1930s and 1940s. She has visited the ranch almost every year since she left it to get married and bring up five children. When Carol and Jim Gardner took over the ranch in the 1980s, Grace was pleased to find they had a profound interest in the ranch's history. They renovated the schoolhouse, rebuilt the log homestead, and required that all new houses on the ranch use log construction. The result is the greatest concentration of fine log homes in the American West. Ted Haynes, Grace's co-author, bought land on the ranch in 1996 and has written extensively on its history and environment.

The primary organization of this narrative is chronologic, starting with the ranch's founder and continuing to the modern ranch. But some subjects like cattle, timber, and the Harper School, fill chapters that span generations. The authors have taken great pains to be accurate, presenting alternate versions of some stories and omitting statements of which they were uncertain.

The authors thank those who have contributed to this history, especially Grace's brother, Claude Vandevert Junior. Other major contributors were David Vandevert, Les Joslin, Vince Vandevert, Carol Gardner, Ed Adams, Janet Jarvis of The Jarvis Group Architects, Pete Newell, Tim and Rene Finnegan, and Kay Culpepper (who drew the ranch maps). Any errors, however, are solely the responsibility of the authors.

Grace remembers how her grandfather, William Plutarch Vandevert, sat on his front porch and told stories about his life and the ranch. If Bill were alive today, he would be pleased to know Vandevert Ranch lives on and he would be delighted to read this book.

CHAPTER 1

Bear Hunter

William Plutarch Vandevert was born in Cottage Grove, Oregon, in the Willamette Valley, in 1854. When he was 15 years old, Bill's uncle, Thomas Clark, persuaded Bill's parents that Bill should help Clark drive 29 horses from Oregon to California. The boy broke his shoulder along the way but came back with three horses of his own, a saddle, and $200 in gold.

Bill's mother had been on one of her brother's horse drives that ended far worse. Grace Clark Vandevert came west along the Oregon Trail in 1851 with her brother Thomas, other members of the Clark family, and about 70 high-quality horses that Thomas expected to sell in Oregon for a big profit. A young Shoshone warrior, appropriately named Has-No-Horse, could not resist Clark's horses. The Indian and his band attacked the Clark Party near the Raft River in Idaho. The raiders stole all the horses, killed Grace's mother and younger brother, and scarred Grace for life.

Grace was expected to die from her wounds before the next day dawned. But she survived and her brother Thomas's wagon train continued west. The traditional story is that they came straight across Oregon to reach the Deschutes River at the future site of the city of Bend. A monument in Pioneer Park in Bend attests that the Clarks were the first European-Americans to camp on the site. This route would have taken them through the same unmapped desert of Eastern Oregon where an 1845 wagon train suffered hardship, thirst, and death in pursuit of the so-called Meek's Cutoff. The alternate story, favored by some serious historians, is that the 1851 party followed the usual Oregon Trail along the Columbia River and it was not until Thomas Clark came west again in 1853 that he camped on the Bend site. In either case, it was Thomas Clark who named Pilot Butte on the east side of Bend, one of only three extinct volcanoes within the city limits of a city in the continental United States.

Later on, in the Willamette Valley, Grace met her brother's business partner, Joshua Jackson Vandervort. Thomas and Joshua had earned the money to buy horses by catching the early days of the California gold rush in 1848. Grace thought Vandervort sounded "too Dutchy" and she required that Joshua change his name to Vandevert when they married in 1853. The couple moved to Cottage Grove, near Eugene, and their first son, William Plutarch Vandevert, known as Bill, was born there on February 24, 1854.

William Plutarch Vandevert.

The Vandeverts had pioneering in their blood. Bill's father Joshua came to Oregon from Ohio. Bill's grandfather, James Madison Vandervort, had emigrated from Virginia to Iowa. Six generations further back, Michael Pauluzen Van der Voort was one of the early settlers of Dutch New Amsterdam (later New York City). Michael owned property on Pearl Street in Manhattan that would be worth hundreds of millions today. Wall Street is named after a wall for which Michael brought the palisades to Manhattan by ship. Michael went on to become one of the first settlers of what is now Maryland.

When Bill Vandevert was 17, two years after his California trip, he left the Willamette Valley with a crew to survey near Summer Lake in eastern Oregon. Bill was probably the youngest member of the crew and the one charged with caring for the horses and washing the pots. After crossing the Cascades, the crew traveled south along the Deschutes River.

The party followed a track called the Huntington Road. The road was built in 1867 by the Oregon Superintendent of Indian Affairs, J.W. Perit Huntington, so the federal government could bring supplies from The Dalles on the Columbia River south to Fort Klamath in fulfillment of treaty obligations to the Klamath Indians. There is a portion of that road, still called Huntington, near Vandevert Ranch today.

About 15 miles south of the future site of Bend, the crew camped for the night in a meadow amid a forest of ponderosa and lodgepole pines. There was a spring in the meadow that ran down to the willows beside the Little Deschutes River. The men watched the sun set south of a mammoth snow-capped volcano. Perhaps the men caught fish for dinner. In all of his later roaming, Bill Vandevert never forgot that evening and that meadow—the future site of Vandevert Ranch.

At age 22, at his Uncle Thomas' urging, Bill took off for Fort Griffen, Texas, to learn the cattle business with a famous company called the Hashknife. He started carrying mail and messages over the wide range where the cattle roamed. He worked his way up to become a herd boss. His job was to watch the men who were watching the cattle.

It was Bill's good fortune in 1878 that Sadie Vincenheller, well educated and fluent in French and Spanish, arrived in Fort Griffen to teach school. When the stagecoach let her out, she knocked on the door of a nearby house to borrow a lantern. Bill Vandevert an-

Sadie Vincenheller as a young woman.

swered the door. The two were married two years later on November 10, 1880 in Sadie's hometown of Jeffersontown, Kentucky.

In 1884, the Hashknife was acquired by the newly formed Aztec Land and Cattle Company. Aztec had bought a million acres in Arizona and New Mexico from the Atlantic and Pacific Railroad. The company contracted 400 railroad cars to bring the Hashknife cattle from Texas. The cars were unloaded all along the line from the New Mexico border to Flagstaff. Aztec had become the third-largest cattle company in North America. Bill and Sadie moved to Holbrook, Arizona, with the company and the cattle.

The East Coast founder of Aztec had seen the land from a train window in a particularly wet year. Dry years, rugged country, and the company's lack of experience made management difficult and rustling a way of life. Zane Grey, the prolific western novelist, immortalized the roughness of Northern Arizona cattle ranching in his novel, *The Hash Knife Outfit*, published in 1933. In the book, the Hash Knife Outfit was a band of outlaw cattle rustlers.

Among Bill's other tasks for Aztec, he built a stable behind the company's new headquarters in Holbrook. Beginning a lifetime of community involvement, Bill helped establish the Chalcedony #6 Masonic Lodge in the town. Fifty years later, the lodge invited him back to celebrate the anniversary of its founding. Over 80 years old and walking with a cane, Bill thought enough of his years in Holbrook to take the train there and back to attend. The lodge gave him an Indian blanket that he kept on his bed for the rest of his life.

By the late 1880s, Aztec's cattle business was declining due to drought and overgrazing. Sadie was getting tired of all the fights between sheep men and cattlemen. She and Bill would have to drag in wounded men from the street and treat them. She was also homesick to see her sister in New York. Perhaps Bill wanted to see what the big city was like. Then a disastrous fire burned most of Holbrook on June 23, 1888. Many residents escaped with only the clothes on their backs. The conflagration may have precipitated the Vandeverts' departure.

By the time they left Arizona, Bill and Sadie had five children in tow. Back east for one year, they lived about 30 miles from New York City, in Spring Valley, Rockland County. Knowing Bill Vandevert, it would be surprising if he did not go hunting in the Adirondacks and the Catskills. But the big city and its environs were probably not to his taste, given where he chose to go next.

Bill's brother, Charlie, wrote to say that he had bought the land on the Little Deschutes that Bill had remembered all these years. The land was 100 miles from the nearest railroad. The Vandeverts could lead a largely self-sufficient life, pit themselves against the wilderness, and be major contributors to whatever community might grow up around them. Best of all, there were bears in the woods.

Bill Vandevert had long ago begun to make his reputation as a bear hunter. He made the San Francisco newspapers in his 20s when he killed a much-feared "Silver Lake Grizzly." This may have been a dwarf sub-species of grizzly known as a lava bear. The hunters who had cornered the bear in a canyon were afraid to go in after it. Bill went in alone. He got so close to the bear before he shot it that the powder from his gun singed the bear's hair. Bill had only been passing by while carrying mail for the Army between Oregon and California.

Bill said his father, Joshua Jackson Vandevert, also loved hunting and dogs. On his way to fetch a minister for his marriage to Grace Clark, Joshua came across two fine hound puppies. "He slipped one into each coat pocket and brought them along," said Bill. "I still hunt bears with the descendants of those puppies."

In the spring of 1892, Bill's family moved to their new ranch on the Little Deschutes, started raising cattle, and began building a log house. Bill paid his brother $600 for two 80-acre parcels on the east side of the Little Deschutes. He homesteaded the adjacent 160 acres that were mostly on the west side of the river. The homesteading laws required that he build a house on the homesteaded land. But Bill wanted to build his house on the east side of the river, where the road between The Dalles and Klamath City went by and there was access to the wider world. He built his house on one of the few pieces of high ground east of the Little Deschutes that was still part of the land he was homesteading. The eastern boundary of the homesteaded land ran right past his front door. The house has been called "The Homestead" or "The Old Homestead" ever since.

Bill salvaged a blacksmith shop, some doors, and perhaps some floorboards from small buildings erected by the previous owners of the two lots he had purchased. He built his log house in stages. In 1892, he first built the south half of a one-story building that ran north-south. This included two rooms that later became the master bedroom and the front hall. In 1895, he built the north half of the north-south building and added a second story and the front porch. In 1909, when Sadie was expecting her daughter, Mittye and her sister, also named Mittye, to visit from the east, Bill added the dining room and kitchen on the back with a bedroom above them. He built the back rooms level with the front of the house. But the front of the house had already settled into the ground. When the back of the house settled the floor in the back was lower than in the front. There were always steps down from one part of the house to the other.

Bill used logs from trees on his the ranch to build the house, mostly lodgepole pine with some ponderosa. He "scribed" the logs (shaped the log tops and bottoms) so each log would fit with the log lying above it and the log lying below it. He used a lot of smaller logs (7" to 9" in diameter) because they would shrink less than large logs and the spaces between the logs would not open up so much. He spiked the logs together with long metal spikes. Ed Adams, an expert log craftsman who worked on most of the modern houses on the ranch, says that Bill Vandevert did an excellent job under the circumstances. Bill had only axes and adzes with possibly a two-person whipsaw. For chinking Bill used mud, straw, and clay—probably mixed with a little horse manure.

Most of the house used full round logs, but Bill squared off the logs in the south half of the long front section of the house. There was still chinking between the logs, but the outside and inside surfaces of the walls in this part of the house, where the master bedroom was, were flat. It was extra work to square off the logs, but it made the outside wall less vulnerable to water damage and it made the inside look more modern and civilized. Sadie probably appreciated that. But sometime before 1912, Bill acquired, from an early sawmill in Bend, slabs cut from the rounded surfaces of logs when the logs were squared up so they could be milled into lumber. These bark-covered slabs were usually sent to the burner so Bill got them for a low price or possibly for free. He nailed them onto the outside of the south part of the house to improve the insulation and protect the logs underneath. At some point in the history of the house, the slabs were removed, probably because they rotted more quickly than the logs beneath them.

Sometime before Grace was born in 1929, boards running vertically were nailed to the interior walls and covered with wallpaper. The ceilings were painted with calcimine, a quick-drying combination of calcium carbonate, water, and glue that was popular in the late 19th and early 20th century. It freshened up surfaces where wood stoves had deposited soot.

From the edge of the wilderness, Bill Vandevert gained a national reputation as a bear hunter and guide. In 1922, he told the *Oregon Journal,* "I took to hunting like a duck takes to water. When I was a youngster, deer and elk and bear were plenty. Two of my mother's brothers—the Clark boys—were bachelors. They were great hunters. When I was a boy, ammunition was expensive and hard to come by. They always saw to it that I was never out of powder or lead." Bill claimed to have killed over 100 bears.

Irvin S. Cobb, a famous American humorist, wrote a story about hunting with Bill that appeared in the May 1922 issue of *Cosmopolitan* magazine. (The magazine has since changed its readership.) The story was called "The Bear that Hunted Me" and it told of a hunt in Newberry Crater where Bill's favorite dog, named Bounce, treed a black bear that Cobb shot and made into a rug. Cobb said the names of all Bill's dogs began with "B" in honor of the lead dog in the pack that had helped scare off Has-No-Horse when the Indians attacked Bill's mother on the Oregon Trail.

In his 1937 book, *Ranger Trails*, John Riis described the days in 1911–1913when he was a pioneer forest ranger at the Big River Ranger Station, just three miles southwest of Vandevert Ranch. One day, his dog scared up a "fat young bear" that Riis figured could feed a lot of people along the river.

"Back at the ranger station, I telephoned the Vandervoort boys on the river road to come up with their bear hounds. They rode over the bridge an hour later accompanied by two business men from Portland up in the hills for a vacation"." After an exciting chase pursuing the dogs and the bear, Riis reports, "There was bear meat for supper that night at Big River and at many a cabin on the river road for the news of the kill spread and we divided the carcass with several visitors."

Among Bill's bear hunting clients was Averell Harriman, who went on to become ambassador to the Soviet Union, supervisor of the Marshall Plan, and governor of the State of New York. Long before Ernest Hemingway wrote about guiding women on hunts, Vandevert guided Anna Crocker of the Crocker family that participated in building the transcontinental railroad. He said she shared her smokes with him.

Bill and Sadie's ranch became a post office and a stagecoach stop. The Vandeverts put travelers up overnight. People with horses and wagons could only travel about 15 to 20 miles a day and it was 15 miles each way to Bend in the north and La Pine to the south. Freighters traveled north and south pulling trains of heavy wagons with large teams of horses. Russ Baehr reports the stopover places were often post offices but "more often were livery barns where teams or mounts could be changed, fed, and watered. Some were bigger than Vandevert's."

Emma Lemon, who stopped at the Homestead on the way from Washington to California in 1898, wrote the area had a "real backwoods" appearance but noted the Vandeverts "had sent their daughter to school in the east." This was the oldest daughter, Mittye, who had stayed in the east with relatives. "They had a little store and a blacksmith shop but were stock raisers for the most part."

In 1898 and 1899, Bill worked for the federal government as a fire guard and a trail blazer in what was then called the Cascade Range Forest Reserve. He would take a pack string into the Cascades from Sisters to North Umpqua and send in reports. He would be gone two weeks, rest a week or so, and go back out again. When a man named Cy J. Bingham was appointed the first official ranger in the reserve, Bill Vandevert was his assistant. Phil Brogan, author of *East of the Cascades,* wrote that the two kept their eyes on distant fires for days "then—if conditions warranted—'took action.' That action generally consisted of a one-man attack on the flames with a shovel and axe."

When he was in Arizona, Bill had guided a man named Alexander M. Drake in the Petrified Forest. Drake visited Central Oregon in 1900 on a leisurely search for good fishing and business opportunities. When Drake stopped his wagon at what was then called Farewell Bend, Bill came by to say hello. Drake and Vandevert did not realize they had met previously until they stood face to face and talked for while. Drake was already thinking about the opportunities for irrigation in the area, but Bill's knowledge of the land and his enthusiasm for it helped Drake make a commitment. He founded the Pilot Butte Development Company and was pumping water through the Pilot Butte Canal by 1904. Irrigation rapidly advanced Bend's prospects and, in December 1904, Bend incorporated itself as a city.

To give his family a taste of adventure and the outside world, Bill took them all to the Lewis and Clark Centennial Exposition of 1905 in Portland. The fair had exhibits from 21 countries and averaged 11,600 visitors a day. Among its attractions were free motion pictures (a novelty in 1905) and the Forestry Building, said to be the world's largest log cabin. Bill's son Claude Senior wrote about the trip.

"We just loaded up two wagons—one a four-horse and the other a two-horse team. It took five days to Salem and two more to Portland. We stayed at Barlow and it rained so hard they let us put our beds in the barn.

"We camped at Guilds Lake (in the Vaughn Street area it would be now). We stayed a week and took in all of the fair and everything and still had a little money left. So we went to the wholesale houses, filled the wagons with food, and came on home. Then, because there was no road from Hood River to The Dalles, we decided we would ship out of Portland on the boat. You had to leave early in the morning so we drove our wagons to the warehouse the night before and slept there. At 5:00 a.m. we loaded them on the boat, *The Dalles City*, and pulled out of Portland at 7:00 a.m. We got to The Dalles at 5:00 that afternoon. They took the two wagons, six horses, and all the family on that boat for $24.50."

Bill Vandevert chose his life on the ranch and he loved it. He once told a reporter, "I have done a lot of roaming in my time, but when a man marries his roaming days are pretty well over. He exchanges the joys of the long trail for the comfort of the home fireside." And, of course, bear hunting, trail blazing, and fire spotting.

One daughter who shot a bear herself, Kathryn Grace, wrote sentimentally of life on the ranch, "Just 18 years ago yesterday we left New York for the wilds of Oregon...How brave Papa and Mama must have been...Here we have lived and grown, strived and struggled together, making ourselves what we are and binding ourselves to one another... It has been 18 years of almost perfect happiness outside of the few little hardships that are bound to come."

Bill turned his cattle over to two of his sons before World War I, but he continued to guide bear hunts. Well into his 60s he boasted, "I can still tire out most young fellows who go out in the hills with me."

Bill lived on his ranch until 1942. He witnessed five births on the ranch and four deaths. He was briefly suspected of murder. But he saw his children, his grandchildren, and all of Central Oregon grow up around him.

CHAPTER 2

Land, Water, and Nature

Vandevert Ranch lies at the north end of what geologists call the La Pine Basin. The 92- mile Little Deschutes River flows through this basin and joins the Deschutes River about a mile north of the ranch. The Cascade Range lies to the west of the ranch and Newberry Caldera to the east. Though the Cascades dominate the landscape of Oregon today, they began to rise only about seven million years ago—a very short time in geology. Newberry is a shield volcano that last erupted, spewing a flow of obsidian, about 1,500 years ago.

Looking west from the ranch toward the Cascade Range.

The La Pine Basin began dropping between the two mountain masses from six hundred thousand to one million years ago. Lava from Newberry started backing up against lava from the Cascade Range about seven hundred thousand years ago, blocking rivers and creating lakes and marshes in the basin. About two hundred thousand years ago, glaciers advancing from the Cascade Range and Newberry Volcano cut rivers that drained the lakes and marshes.

Looking east from the ranch toward Newberry Caldera and Paulina Peak.

But Benham Lake was formed about 5050 BC when lava blocked the Deschutes River west of Lava Butte. Benham Lake covered what is now Sunriver, Crosswater, and much of the ranch until about 1,900 years ago. Then the river broke through the lava and formed Benham Falls. The reports from drilling a 100-foot well near the schoolhouse on the ranch show volcanic rock alternating with levels of sand, gravel, boulders, and clay deposited by water.

At a deeper geologic level, the ranch lies at the western edge of the High Lava Plains Province of Oregon. The thousand-foot-deep aquifer from which nearby Sunriver draws its water runs perpendicular to the north-south Deschutes River Valley and extends east all the way to Burns. Two hundred million years ago the ranch sat on the floor of the Pacific Ocean.

Except near the Little Deschutes River, the top layer of organic matter in the soil on the ranch is less than an inch thick and less than 7,000 years old. This layer is the product of forests that have experienced periodic fires. Going further down, the next two to five feet of soil is volcanic ash (very small bits of rock and glass, similar to sand) from the eruption of Mt. Mazama (Crater Lake) about 7,700 years ago (5650 BC). The wind was blowing to the northeast when Mt. Mazama blew its top so much of the ash fell on Vandevert Ranch area. Thin layers of Mazama ash exist as far away as Saskatchewan. The sand-like soil drains rapidly. While the ground surface is very dry during the summer and fall, the water table, reflecting the proximity of the Little Deschutes River and the Deschutes River, is only five feet below the surface throughout the ranch.

The old log homestead at the ranch lies at about the same latitude as Cottage Grove in the Willamette Valley and Jackson Hole in Wyoming. The ranch's climate is great for people. Summer brings many clear days with low humidity and daytime high temperatures in the 70°s. Of the 22 annual inches of precipitation (about the same as the San Francisco Bay Area), 46% falls in November through January, which is great for skiing and a white Christmas.

But plants have to be tough to survive on the ranch. Frost can occur at any time of the year. In the summer, the ground heats up rapidly on sunny days and loses heat quickly in the evening. The growing season averages only 70 to 80 days. The positive side of a climate that is hard on plants is that it limits the variety of weeds and pests that can live on the ranch. An important advantage for the Vandevert family was that the area was almost completely free of cattle diseases and, apparently,

Zig-zag fence of the type used by the Vandeverts. Logs were stacked without nails.

very healthy for settlers. Grace says, "I had no allergies—didn't even know what the word meant. I had a cousin who came to the ranch every summer and never had the awful asthma that she had in Indiana."

The ranch is primarily a mixed lodgepole ("jack pine") and ponderosa ("yellow pine") forest, though the original forests around it were mostly ponderosa, which is especially valuable for lumber. Claude Vandevert Senior told Russ Baehr, "We passed up huge stands of yellow pine to settle on the more open jack pine and bitterbrush lands we needed for cattle feed." The cattle would eat bitterbrush, the grass that grew between the lodgepoles and, of course, the grass in the meadows and in the riparian areas.

Lodgepole pines were so plentiful that the Vandeverts stacked lodgepole logs to make zig-zag fences along the east and west sides of the ranch and along the north border. Pastures within the ranch were separated by post-and-rail fences or by barbed wire. There were no gates between the pastures. The Vandeverts took the rails down when they needed to move the cattle. There are still post-and-rail fences on the ranch today but no zig-zag fences. Buck-and-rail fences, with a few horizontal logs nailed to bucks—logs crossed in the vertical plane like X's—are common throughout the West, but they were not used on the ranch until the 1990s."

The dominant understory shrubs are wild currant and bitterbrush. There is a naturally occurring meadow east of the river and a pasture, cleared by a fire in 1990, west of the river. These and a few smaller upland areas are largely grass and rabbit brush.

A wide riparian area dominated by willows and grasses winds through the center of the ranch from south to north. The natural pattern of stream flows in the Little Deschutes would reach high water in May as the winter snow melted and very low water in August and September due to the lack of summer rains. Actual flow differs because substantial water is stored in Crescent Lake (the dam was built in 1922) and released for irrigation in the summer. Crescent Creek, which flows out of Crescent Lake, brings more water to its confluence with the Little Deschutes than do the headwaters of the Little Deschutes.

The Little Deschutes River flows for two miles through the ranch.

According to many reports, there were more fish in the rivers than there are today. Leona Stocking wrote of her relatives in the area, "There were always lots of trout in the Deschutes and Arnold (born 1903) remembers using a willow pole and a fly hook to catch them."

The Deschutes Water Alliance's report on instream flows in the Deschutes Basin states, "Bull trout historically spawned in the Little Deschutes River and its tributaries, but they have been extirpated from this reach." Bull trout, a type of char, are very similar in appearance to Dolly Varden trout.

> "Until the early 1930s, the fish in the river were almost exclusively rainbow trout," says Claude Vandevert Junior. "I remember the first German Brown we caught. We didn't know what it was, so we took it to the Fish and Game Commission in Bend to identify it. After that, they rapidly expanded. There were only a few Dolly Varden. Dad would fish specifically for them during the high water season in the mouths of inlets to the sloughs. They seemed to lie there eating the minnows that were going in and out of the sloughs. About every three years, the whitefish would school up into the river as part of their reproductive cycle. Since they were a trash fish, there was no limit on them and we could snag them with triple hooks. We would catch about a washtub full and then smoke them. Even though they were very bony, smoking them made them crisp and we could eat them, bones and all."

Claude's sister, Mary Jean, wrote,

"In my time (the 1930s and 1940s), there were just trout: German browns, rainbows, whitefish, and, a long time ago, Dolly Varden. I don't really remember them, but I've heard enough to know they were *big*. The biggest fish I remember was one my Dad caught at Pringle Falls on the Big Deschutes. He drew an outline of it on a piece of lumber that was near the river and it was almost exactly three feet long. I believe it was a German brown. Dad (Pop to me) was an expert fly fisherman. He and my older brother Claude tied their own flies. Pop would go out in the early evening when the shadows were just coming out over the river by the willows and, within minutes, he usually had our supper. Pop was a 'Fly Fisherman'! He sometimes would use a worm or a grasshopper, but he rather looked down on anyone who thought fishing was something where you sit on a bridge or the bank of the river and just wait for the fish to come to you. "My favorite fish memory is the summer that we had a school of about five or six big German browns that actually became tame enough to come and eat bread from my hand while I sat on the steps going down into the river. Believe it or not, a couple of them would let me stroke their backs as they swam in place there. Instead of a dog paddle I suppose you would call it a fish paddle. Anyway, Pop thought it was pretty neat that I 'tamed' those fish. They didn't come back the next summer. I'm afraid someone wanted to eat them rather than feed them."

Information about the current trout population in the river is anecdotal. The past ranch foreman reported seeing both brown and rainbow trout in the river. The trout were sometimes visible from the bridge on the ranch and were spotted darting away during bank restoration work.

The most avid and knowledgeable fisherman on the ranch today reports, "I walk the river all the time. I see fish significantly over two pounds in the river all year except in July and August when the river warms up. In July and August, I only see fish in the four to seven inch range. It seems one can only catch large fish when the water is cooler. I did catch a four-pound brown trout in my backyard at the very end of May 2007."

In 2005, the Oregon Department of Fish and Wildlife reported that early land clearing destabilized the stream and decreased its complexity. Stream complexity (i.e., the variety of environments within the river) is beneficial for fish. Cattle grazing prevented the recovery of the eroded banks. Gradually sloped banks do not provide a good fish habitat and continuous erosion yields sediment that fills the spaces in the gravel where the fish lay their eggs. Bank restoration work by the current owners and the passage of time should help improve the trout habitat and increase the fish population.

Wildlife species have come and gone on the ranch. There were no quail when Claude and Grace Vandevert were growing up in the 1930s. The birds were then widely introduced throughout Central Oregon and are now common on the ranch. The expansion of the willows since cattle grazing ceased in 1971 has favored the quail. Perhaps the changes in grazing and willows explain why desert cottontail rabbits have appeared on the ranch since the 1930s and 1940s.

Elk grazing in the horse pasture.

Claude Vandevert Junior says, "There were no beaver until maybe the middle 1930s when a very few began to show up. Then occasionally we would see a beaver house but never dams; the river was too big for them to try that. There were a lot of muskrats and mink and Dad did a lot of trapping to make an income. But these, too, began to disappear. The muskrats fed on the freshwater mussels and finally ate them all and left." Any muskrat resurgence would first appear in the sloughs and backwaters, but there are no signs of muskrats on the ranch at this time. There are very few mink, but a big dark male lives near the bridge.

There is only one known beaver on the ranch today yet there may be a few more.

"We had ducks and geese not only to eat, but to sleep on," wrote Mary Jean. "Not just down pillows but down mattresses. I doubt that any guests we had thought of us as poor after the meals we had and the luxurious beds they slept on!" Ducks and geese still nest on the ranch every year, especially near the pond that was dug in the early 1990s.

The ranch is an excellent environment for many animals. Timber, brush, and willow patches provide plenty of cover. Food is abundant in grasses and shrubs for browsers. Birds have a good variety of seeds. Animals that live year-round on the ranch include coyotes, river otters, porcupines, desert cottontail rabbits, gray squirrels, yellow pine chipmunks, and golden-mantled ground squirrels. The ranch is a transitory range for mule deer and elk. A few bears appeared in the area in the 1980s and early 1990s but have not been seen since. Cougars were gone from the area for a long time but are starting to come back.

Birds that raise their broods on the ranch include great-horned owls, red-tailed hawks, mallards, cinnamon teals, wood ducks, flickers, blue jays, and Canada geese. Other birds frequently seen on the ranch include ospreys, great blue herons, kingfishers, ravens, red-winged blackbirds, and other varieties of hawks and owls.

CHAPTER 3

Oregon Frontier

Central Oregon was one of the last frontiers in the lower 48 states, and even the Indians did not live there during most of the year. They came and hunted and some tribes, like the Klamaths, traveled through area near Vandevert Ranch on their way to the great Indian trading center at Celilo Falls on the Columbia River. The ranch may have been a favorite camping place because of the grass and willows for the horses to eat. Many arrowheads have been found on the ranch, particularly south of the rock pile by the entrance. When the Indians

Claude Vandevert Junior's collection of arrowheads from the ranch. The ranch was a popular camping place for the Indians.

camped on the Deschutes near its source, they leaned logs together and covered the structures with mats woven from tule grass. Early ranchers, and perhaps Bill Vandevert himself, named the area that is now Wickiup Reservoir after these Indian shelters.

The first whites to see the area around Vandevert Ranch were Hudson's Bay trappers led by Peter Skene Ogden in November 1826. They rode up the Newberry Volcano into the Newberry Crater from the east, watered their horses, and came down the west side. From there, they could see the land where the ranch is today.

The next white man in the area was Nathaniel Wyeth in 1834. He and a few companions used canoes to explore the upper Deschutes and its tributaries in December of that year. There was four feet of snow on the ground, but the men camped upriver as far as Pringle Falls. They might have paddled up the Little Deschutes to look around.

The region always had its advantages. John C. Fremont, leading a federally sponsored exploration from the Columbia River south to the Klamath marshes and on to California in late 1843, wrote of "the beautiful pine forest, the deep and swift Deschutes, and the bottomlands of lush grass."

But Central Oregon was hard to reach. It took years to find the few difficult passes over the Cascades from the west. The few brave pioneers coming directly across Oregon from the east, instead of along the Columbia River, struggled to find water along the way.

To evaluate a north-south route for a railroad between the Columbia River and Sacramento on the American River in California, Secretary of War Jefferson Davis commissioned an 1855 survey of the Deschutes River area. Members of the survey party were Lieutenants Henry Abbot and Robert Williamson (namesake of the Williamson River near Klamath Lake), Dr. John Newberry (Newberry Crater), George Crook (Crook County), and Philip Sheridan (a famous Union general in the Civil War). The conclusion of the survey was discouraging: "It will be seen that the Deschutes Valley is mostly a barren region, furrowed by immense canyons, and offering very few inducements to settlers. Its few fertile spots, excepting those in the immediate vicinity of The Dalles, are separated from the rest of the world by almost impassable barriers, and nature seems to have guaranteed it forever to the wandering savage and the lonely seeker after the wild and sublime in natural scenery."

In order to avoid having to defend the Central Oregon wilderness, The Army issued an order in 1856 forbidding immigrants to locate east of the Cascades. The order was revoked two years later when the Army decided it would be harder to keep the whites out than to control the Indians.

If early Central Oregon could not attract settlers, it could attract miners. Gold was discovered in 1861 in Canyon City, about 120 miles east of the Deschutes River. When traffic picked up between The Dalles and Canyon City, the Shoshone Indians (known to whites as the Snakes) turned some of their attention away from attacking immigrants on the Oregon Trail and toward to raiding the goods-laden wagons heading to the gold mines. Until 1865, when the Civil War ended, the U.S Army's response was sporadic.

The Shoshone had not always been enemies of the whites. Sacajawea was a Shoshone and her tribe had provided essential assistance to Lewis and Clark 60 years earlier. Hostilities escalated into the so-called Snake War of 1864–1868. The growing flow of new settlers put stress on the Indians. The Indians increased their raids on wagon trains, leading the whites to clamor for more action by the Army. There were no large battles in the Snake War, but rather a succession of raids back and forth between the adversaries. The Indians on the Warm Springs Reservation were allies of the Army and enemies of the Shoshone. They were often more aggressive than the Army in pursuing and fighting the enemy. In turn, however, the Warm Spring Reservation suffered devastating Shoshone raids.

Various bands of Shoshone operated independently. Teanamad of the Walpapi band, known to the whites as Chief Paulina, inflicted more damage, death, and fear than any other Shoshone. He stole cattle and horses, burned houses, and killed settlers all across Central Oregon. He brought death to many travelers on the road between The Dalles and Canyon City. The growing economy of Canyon City collapsed and Central Oregon was almost completely abandoned by settlers.

One of the last stage stations still operating between The Dalles and Canyon City belonged to James Clark. James was an older brother of Grace Clark, Bill Vandevert's mother and survivor of the "Clark Massacre" of 1851. In 1866, Chief Paulina looted and burned James Clark's stage station, known thereafter as "Burnt Ranch." In April 1867, Chief Paulina stole cattle from another stage station. Clark spotted the chief and fetched Howard Maupin to help pursue the band to a camp on Trout Creek. The two men crept close to the camp and began shooting. Most of the Indians scattered but Chief Paulina was shot to death and his body left to decay. Some versions of the story say that Maupin killed him. Others say Maupin wounded him and Clark, recognizing the chief as the man who burned his ranch, finished him off.

In the 1990s, Allen Jacobs took a metal detector into the rocky corner where Chief Paulina died and found casings and slugs. A rifle test on Maupin's Henry rifle, not fired for at least 92 years, showed that two of the slugs Jacobs found with human blood on them were from Maupin's rifle. Another slug with blood on it was a .50 caliber, compatible with Clark's .56-.50 Spencer rifle. Both rifles were repeaters, a new technology at the time that allowed the firing of multiple shots without reloading. The repeating rifles allowed the outnumbered Maupin and Clark to drive off Chief Paulina's band and kill him.

Chief Paulina was so famous that more places in Central Oregon are named for him than for anyone else. One such place, Paulina Peak at the south end of Newberry Crater, can be seen from Vandevert Ranch. One lot on the ranch was named Paulina because of its excellent view of the peak. After hearing Grace, the co-author of this book, describe Paulina as "a very bad man," the owners gained permission to change the name of their lot.

The Snake War came to an end in 1868. The first whites to take advantage of the peace were cattle and sheep men who could graze large herds on vast expanses of grass and scrub north and east of the future site of Bend. The land was dry and the grazing was sometimes sparse but the government-owned rangeland had one big advantage: It was free. The animals could walk long distances to market, instead of being hauled by railroads. Cattle raised in central and eastern Oregon were driven not just to The Dalles but to the San Francisco Bay Area and even as far as Cheyenne, Wyoming. Cattle and sheep dominated the region in the 1880s and 1890s.

Prineville, in the rangeland about 30 miles northeast of Bend, was the first town incorporated in Central Oregon and was the leading municipality in the region from its founding in 1877 until Bend's population exploded with the arrival of the railroad in 1911.

The area around Vandevert Ranch was not well suited to large cattle herds. Too much of the terrain was woodland and not enough was grassland. But 80 acres of meadow were just about right for a man who wanted to support himself and perhaps sell the land at a profit. Before Bill Vandevert took them over in 1892, one 80-acre parcel east of the Little Deschutes belonged to a homesteader named Scoggin and another belonged to a man remembered as "Dutch John." This Dutch John was very likely John Felderwerd for whom Dutch Flat near Mount Bachelor is named. Scoggin had a small house on his land and at least five acres in farmland.

There was a spring on the hillside about 50 yards above where the log Homestead is now. The spring gave rise to stream that went down to the river. The border between the two 80-acre parcels went right near the spring.

Scoggin and Dutch John both thought they owned the spring or perhaps one of them owned the land below the spring and felt entitled to the water flowing from it. The more they thought about using the land, the more important the spring became. There being a shortage of law, courts, and judges in the area, the two decided to settle their dispute by fighting a duel. But as soon as Scoggin shot and wounded Dutch John, he regretted the whole thing. He went to get help for his bleeding neighbor.

Scoggin rode 50 miles to Prineville to bring back a doctor. Dutch John recovered and both men decided to leave their properties behind. Scoggin moved to the Willamette Valley. Dutch John later built a cabin near the future site of Bend. One day in the early 1900s, he simply disappeared. There were no lawmen in the area and the matter was never investigated. Perhaps a new duel turned out even worse for him than the first one.

The spring over which a duel was fought in approximately 1890. This photo, with the early Homestead in the background, was taken prior to 1923.

More than 100 years later, a man related to the Scoggins bought a lot on Vandevert Ranch and built a log house with his wife. The house overlooked the meadow where the spring once ran. Another relative, whose grandmother was a Scoggin, was the building contractor for the house on another lot.

CHAPTER 4

Pioneer Family

Sadie Vincenheller was 20 years old when the first Kentucky Derby ran near her home and she may well have seen the race. She was born on October 27, 1854, and raised in Bluegrass Country. She undoubtedly knew a good horse when she saw one. Perhaps she was a good judge of horsemen as well.

Sadie Vincenheller as a girl in Kentucky.

Sadie and Bill Vandevert were married in Sadie's hometown, Jeffersontown, Kentucky, on November 11, 1880, when they were both 26. They returned to Texas after marrying and moved on to the frontier cattle country of Arizona. They spent one year in New York with Sadie's sister before moving to Oregon to stay.

On top of running the Homestead and raising her many children, Sadie persuaded the federal government to let her open a post office at the ranch in 1893. It helped that Sadie was a Democrat and that the administration was headed by a Democrat, President Grover Cleveland. Sadie named the post office "Carlisle" after John Griffin Carlisle, a former congressman from Kentucky. Carlisle became Speaker of the

House and then President Cleveland's Secretary of the Treasury. The post office was later moved and renamed "Lava." Sadie took it back for a while before it was discontinued.

It is likely that Sadie, the experienced teacher, supplemented the children's schoolroom education by teaching them at home. The Big Meadows School District was organized on July 21, 1887, and school was held in a log building. Among the pupils after 1892 were most of the Vandevert children. The location remembered by two of the boys 70 years later was about 100 yards southeast of the present day Sunriver Lodge.

As the number of students in the area, and the amount local residents could pay, rose and fell between the 1890s and the 1920s, school was variously held at a school building, at different homesteads, or not at all. The schoolteachers often received room and board in the homes of their students, rotating between the families. The Big Meadows School had more students in its first few years than for many years afterwards because a surge of families started to homestead nearby but then moved on.

The Vandevert Family in 1895. From left to right, Kathryn Grace, Claude Senior, Clint, Thomas William, George, Bill, Arthur (in carriage), Maude, and Sadie. Mittye was in school in New York when the photo was taken.

In 1900–1901, school was held for 18 weeks at Vandevert Ranch. In 1905, a number of parents, including Sadie, moved to Bend so the younger children would be able to attend school for nine months. Sadie brought the family cow with some of the family furniture and rented a house in Bend. Sadie's daughter Maude taught school for six weeks in 1905 in the home of one of the area settlers. In 1909 and 1910, another of Sadie's daughters, Kathryn Grace, taught two 12-week terms in the attic of another settler's house.

Sometime before 1915, the school at Big Meadows was abandoned and a new school was established where a town named Harper was expected to be built near present-day Caldera Springs. In 1925, a new one-room schoolhouse was built near Harper and, in 1929, the building was moved to Vandevert Ranch where it remains to this day. The history of the Harper School appears in its own chapter later in this book.

When most of the Vandevert Children were ready for high school, Bend High School did not exist. It graduated its first class in 1909 and only the three youngest, George, Claude Senior, and Arthur, were Bend High School graduates. Mittye, the eldest daughter, attended high school in New York State where she had remained when the rest of the family moved to Oregon. Four of the children, Thomas William (referred to as "Uncle Bill" in this book), Maude, Clint, and Kathryn Grace left home to attend high school in Salem where Willamette University had a high school program for children from the remote parts of Oregon.

It is a testament to the family's belief in education that, out of the wilderness, three of the sons went on to become doctors and two of the daughters became teachers. A testament to all the children's love of their family and of the ranch is the fact that all of the children spent much of their adult lives on or near the ranch, except for Arthur who brought his family all the way from Kentucky every summer to visit.

Clint (Dr. J. C. Vandevert (1887–1967) completed college at Willamette and continued his education at the University of Oregon Medical School in Portland. He returned to Bend in 1914 and practiced medicine there for 50 years. Grace remembers,

"Whenever any of the family would come to Bend in later years, people would tell us about 'Doc' Van—how he helped set a broken arm, sewed up a shoulder wound, even took care of a stabbing in La Pine. Everyone liked and respected him. His first office was in the O'Kane Building on Oregon Avenue, and then he bought the brick clinic on Franklin Ave behind the old post office that he used for years.

"Uncle Doc was an avid hunter and always had a bird dog close by. He was appointed to the Oregon State Game Commission and was State President of Oregon Trapshooters. He was married to Harriet Dolsen and their two children, Jack and Joan, were raised in a beautiful home above the Deschutes River in downtown Bend. It was a wonderful place to visit for the whole family.

"My Uncle Doc lived on Brooks Street just to the south of Pine Tavern. He was a favorite uncle of all of us. He took time to chat with us when we had to come to his office, although we were told by my mother not to bother him. He always had a few people in his waiting room and when we went into his surgery, he would pick me up and set me on his surgery table and start asking questions about the ranch—how was the fishing—how many new calves this spring—and so on. I realize now that Uncle Doc was a very young man when he first came there and he had to help with the ranching just like Claude, Dave, and me. His house had the most beautiful ponderosa pines and one huge weeping willow tree on the lawn that ran down to the river. It was gorgeous. The house was a hospital to start and then a wonderful home when Uncle Doc lived there. It was huge. At least in those days it was. They tore the house down and made a parking lot out of it about 25 years ago after Uncle Doc died."

In the 1920s and 1930s, Clint owned 80 acres and a cabin at the southeast corner of what is now South Century Drive and Vandevert Road. He and his family came down from Bend on weekends and stayed there while they were visiting the ranch.

George (1888–1972) was in Bend High School's first graduating class in 1909. He went to Willamette University and then worked for a time in the office of the Brooks-Scanlon Lumber Company in Bend.

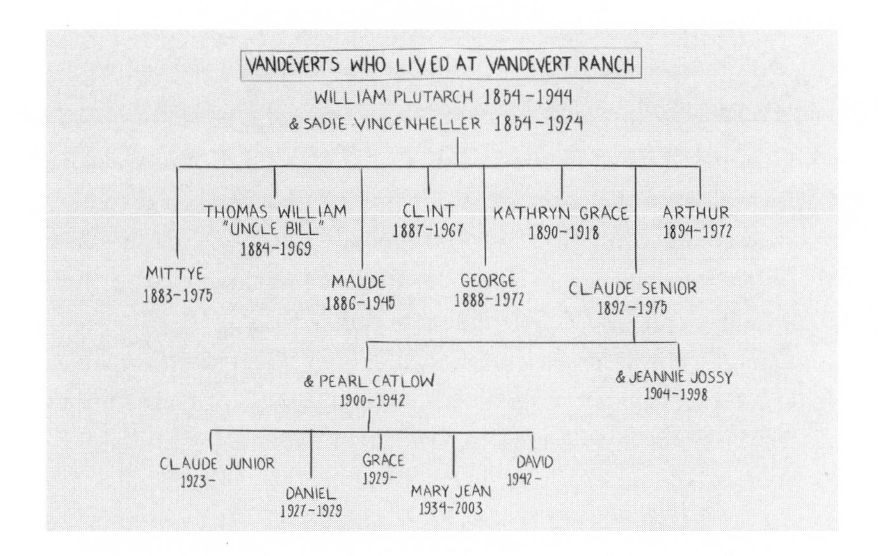

George's son Vince remembers,

"When Dad came down with acute appendicitis it was the sudden relief of pain through surgery that led him to become a doctor. He then went through the University of Oregon Medical School and did his internship and residency in surgery at Good Samaritan Hospital in Portland. He married Olgamarie Paulsen, a Good Samaritan operating room nurse, in 1922. The two spent their honeymoon in a cabin on Wizard Island in Crater Lake National Park. Grampa's connections through the Forest Service must have arranged it. After my father established my mother in a small house in Bend, he did post-graduate work in surgery at Columbia-Presbyterian Hospital in New York City. He returned to Bend and began his practice with Uncle Clint.

"While at Columbia-Presbyterian, he learned about a new thing called baby formula that used condensed milk and several nutritional additives. It was just what he needed when he was faced with my mother's lack of milk and my incessant crying—which led to surgery for double hernia. At that time, unpasteurized milk was delivered to outlying logging camps in five- or 10-gallon cans. The cans sat for hours in the sun on the logging trains. Infant mortality was high. My father taught the women to use canned baby formula for their infants and canned Carnation milk for the older kids. Infant mortality dropped and the families remembered my father fondly for the rest of their lives. I like to say I was the first Carnation Baby in Bend, but I have no proof."

George left Bend in 1930 to set up his own practice in Oakland, California, where he spent most of his career. He lived in Piedmont and had an office in downtown Oakland. He had a second office near the waterfront where he served the Black community two or three nights a week and did not charge them if they were poor.

George's three sons—Vincent, Allan, and George—grew up in Oakland. He moved to Grants Pass, Oregon, and lived there until he died in November 1972. He was buried in Bend near his family.

Arthur (1894–1972) was called "Bush" or "Uncle Bush" all of his life by his family because he was born with a great bushy head of red hair. After graduating from Bend High School, he went to Willamette for pre-med. His mother wanted one of her sons to practice in her home state of Kentucky. So Arthur got his medical degree from the University of Louisville. He went into the hills of Kentucky to practice medicine and there he met his future wife, Martha Shadburn Whitcomb. They were married and moved to Sellersburg, Indiana, across the Ohio River from Louisville. They had two daughters, Sallie Bird and Cynthia. The family came west to visit the ranch frequently in the summertime. Arthur and Sallie Bird wrote a poem about a small stream that ran into Devil's Lake in the High Cascades.

The Little Tyee

I have heard the song of the rivers
That flow leisurely down to the sea,
But this is the song of a brooklet—
The song of the little Tyee.

Nestled away in the great Cascades
Who, glacier clad as they be,
Give of their melting waters
To cool the little Tyee.

It flows not deep nor leisurely,

But splashes and bubbles with glee.
It's a sparkling, laughing river—
This happy little Tyee.

On the moss-covered banks are pine trees
That shelter this rivulet so free,
Their shade is soft and grassy
On the banks of the little Tyee.

Waters as cold as the northland,
As pure as waters can be.
A gift God denied the city
Is the beautiful little Tyee.

I may live forever and ever,
And travel o'r many a sea,
But the memory always shall linger
Of the peace by the little Tyee.

—Arthur and Sallie Bird Vandevert

Arthur was the physician for the Louisville Cement Company in New Albany, Indiana, where he worked until his sight was impaired. He then had an office in Sellersburg where he could diagnose patients. Martha would be his "chauffeur" when he was called out from his home. The couple planned to retire and come back the ranch in Oregon. They wanted to build a home by the rock pile on the hill and live the rest of their lives there. Due to the war and to the changes on the ranch in the 1940s, they had to remain in Indiana. They still visited the ranch as much as they were able and he died in 1972 in Jeffersonville.

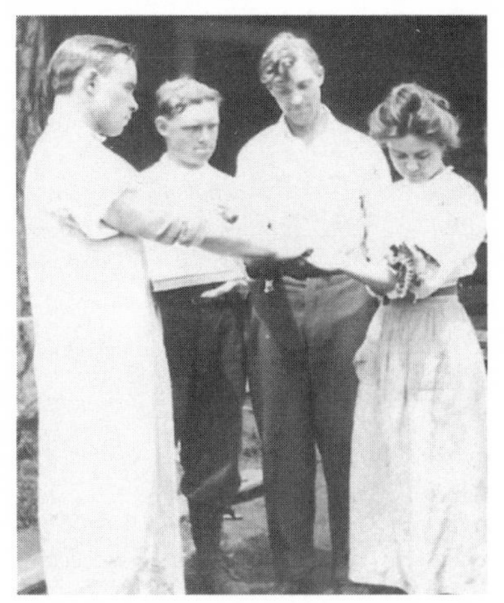

Maude's mock wedding before the real thing. Clint at left is officiating. Uncle Bill is next, then Chet Catlow and Maude.

In 1891, when the rest of the family moved to Oregon, Mittye (1883–1975), the eldest child, stayed in New York State with an aunt and uncle on her mother's side. She was only eight years old at the time. She went on, however, to earn a Master's Degree from Columbia in religious education. She was dedicated to the church and never married. She lived in the South and in California before moving to Bend.

Maude (1886–1945) finished high school at Willamette University in Salem. She went on to college at Willamette, one of the earliest coeducational institutions in the United States. She got her teaching certificate at Oregon State Normal School at Monmouth, about 15 miles west of Salem. The school is now called Western Oregon University. Maude taught school in Summer Lake, Bend, Portland, and La Pine, as well as in the Shevlin-Hixon lumber camps near the ranch.

On June 25, 1912, when she was 26, Maude married Chester Catlow at the Homestead. Maude was the first of three Vandeverts to marry a member of the Catlow family. Chet and Maude had three children—Bill, Betty, and Kathryn. Chet was a musician and played organ music to accompany silent movies in theaters in Portland. In the

Maude Vandevert's wedding to Chester Catlow on June 25, 1912 at the Homestead. Seated left to right, Sadie, Bill, Maude, and Chet. Standing Uncle Bill, Mittye, George, Clint, Arthur, Kathryn Grace, and Claude Senior.

1930s, he left to teach music on St. Lucia, an island country in the Caribbean. He was much beloved by his students and died there in 1974. Maude died in Bend in 1945.

Kathryn Grace (1890–1918) lived only 28 years and spent almost her entire life on the ranch. She died in the influenza epidemic of 1918 and is the only person buried on the ranch. She received a teaching degree from Monmouth Normal School near Salem and taught near the ranch. She was working at the post office in Bend when she died. Though she never married and left no children, she provided a special insight for those who came after her by leaving a diary. The authors of this book wish that she had written more about life on the ranch but can only sympathize with her disappointment in having to put off going away to school, her lack of friends she could confide in, her wish to go to business school instead of into teaching, and her harsh criticism of her own nature. She came to loathe housework and even wished she could take an active role in World War I like a man. But she enjoyed her nieces and nephews. She did have her happier moments and she loved to go out riding on the ranch.

Kathryn Grace Vandevert, Girl of the West.

Grace says, "Kathryn Grace was a lady of very mixed emotions—up one day and down the next. She just couldn't seem to realize that she was such a wonderful person—that her brothers and sisters loved her dearly as did her mother Sadie—and she just put herself down as not being worthy. I would love to have known her. She was a real 'Girl of the West.'"

Two of Bill and Sadie's sons made lives out of raising cattle like their father. The stories of Uncle Bill and Claude Senior will be told in the chapter on the ranchers.

CHAPTER 5

Cattle

Vandevert Ranch was a good place to raise cattle, with two miles of river that flowed year-round. The two types of grass that grew on the ranch provided a balanced diet. Bunchgrass, common throughout dry eastern Oregon, grew on the higher ground in the woodlands and meadow. Bunch grass came back well from being eaten because it grew roots six feet deep that could reach down to water. The cattle got more volume from the clump at the base of the bunch grass than they did from the stalks. Tall green turf grass grew by the river and did not need such deep roots. It had pods about the same size as a fist and provided the cattle with nutrients different from the bunch grass.

The chief advantage of the area was that it was about as free of cattle diseases as any place in the West. Beneficially for people today, there is no Lyme disease or West Nile disease anywhere in the area. Horses occasionally pick up ticks, but people walk everywhere on the ranch without encountering them.

Bill Vandevert was a jack-of-all-trades and did not intend to support his family entirely by raising cattle. He had fewer than 50 head. His grandson, Claude Junior, says Bill was not going to let cattle get in the way of bear hunting. But there were other reasons for Bill limiting his investment in cattle at that time. He had seen the decline of his employer's cattle business in Arizona due to overgrazing and price decreases. According to Jimmy Skaggs in his book *Prime Cut,* the price of live cattle fell to $2.40 per hundredweight in 1886, then to $1.80

in 1887—the lowest price between the Civil War and World War I. In the disastrous winter of 1886–1887, ranchers in north central states lost five times as many cattle as usual to deep snow and extremely low temperatures. The cattle that survived were emaciated. In 1892, cattle looked like a very risky enterprise.

By second decade of the 1900s, the land and cattle business in the Bend area looked a bit better. National cattle prices had recovered to over $5.00 per hundredweight. In 1919, they reached $9.97. After the advent of irrigation in 1904 and the arrival of the railroad in 1911, Bend was booming. The railroad made it possible to market local cattle to the wider world. Bill and Sadie's eldest son, Thomas William (called Uncle Bill), started a new ranch on Paulina Prairie in about 1913 where he grew clover and raised cattle. It was located near La Pine on the east side of Huntington Road. A younger son, Claude Senior, returned from his job with an electric utility company near Portland to take over the original Homestead ranch.

The brothers worked together and ran the two ranches as a single business for 20 years. They expanded the combined herd to about 300 head, about half at the Homestead and half at Uncle Bill's ranch. At some point, Uncle Bill acquired the ranch next to his at Paulina Prairie. Claude bought the nearby Reece place south of the bridge that crosses Paulina Creek on the road up to Paulina Lake. The brothers took cattle to the Reece place to graze at times and also did some haying. In 1934, Uncle Bill moved to Tumalo, selling his original ranch and his share of the business. Claude kept the Reece place and the other La Pine ranch until a minister from California named Jesse Kellems bought both of them in the 1930s and built a rather grand house on what he called Kelldano Ranch. Claude sold all the cattle in 1943 but brought in a smaller herd after World War II.

The first cattle on Vandevert Ranch were Durhams, now known better as Shorthorns. Durhams were a standard breed in Oregon at the time. The chief advantage of the breed was that it grew quickly to full size in two-and-a-half years. It was a good "rustler," meaning it could fend for itself on the range without a lot of looking after. Butchers liked the volume of good cuts of meat they could get from the Durham's squared-off hindquarters. The Durham produced a good volume of milk, which was good for raising strong calves and providing milk for the Vandevert family.

In the 1930s, in the Great Depression, consumer tastes changed to smaller cuts of meat. The ranch migrated the herd toward Herefords by bringing in Hereford bulls to impregnate the cows. Herefords reproduce rapidly, are hardy in winter, and are even easier to handle than Durhams. They are not as good rustlers and their hindquarters do not produce as many high-priced cuts of beef.

The ranch purchased purebred bulls from Sid Stearns, who had a larger cattle operation, to improve the stock. The purebreds were more vulnerable to disease than the other cattle and the Vandeverts preferred to keep their herd somewhat mixed. The ranch had one bull for every 20 to 25 cows. They replaced the bulls every two years so the bulls would not interbreed with the calves they had sired. The male calves were castrated and grew up to be steers rather than bulls. The steers were sold as soon as they were big enough. The cows were kept longer but the herd was about half and half steers and cows at any given time.

The Herefords were a mix of horned and genetically hornless or "polled" cattle. The advantage of polled cattle was that when the steers got into fights they rarely injured each other. In the 1950s and 1960s, when Claude Senior was tending the cattle by himself, he raised only polled cattle to avoid injuries when he was not keeping an eye on them.

In the early days under Bill Vandevert, the cattle grazed on the ranch year-round, supplemented with hay in the winter. But when the combined herd grew to 300 head under the management of Bill's sons, the cattle needed more feed. Starting after 1913, the herd spent the summer together at Crane Prairie, 20 miles west of the ranch and close to the crest of the Cascade Mountain Range. Crane Prairie encompassed about 5,000 acres of grass where three rivers, including the upper reaches of the Deschutes, came together. Not only was the grazing good for the cattle, it gave the rye and grass in the ranch meadows time to grow.

In 1922, a dam was built just below Crane Prairie to store water for irrigation. The reservoir created one of the best fisheries in the northwest, but it obliterated the pasture. At the same time, the U.S. Forest Service offered to lease land for summer grazing from Spring River north almost to Benham Falls. This land was less than five miles from the ranch and the Vandeverts took the Forest Service up on its offer. It meant they could check on the cattle and be home for dinner, instead of spending a day riding to Crane Prairie and a day riding back.

Spring River rises out of the ground into a pool west of the Deschutes and north of the ranch. Its cold waters flow less than a mile north to merge with the Deschutes. The area had been logged so there was sunlight to grow grass. The timber company had used railroads to transport the logs out of the forest and the abandoned rail beds made it easy for the Vandeverts to get to the cattle. The men drove the cattle over the Harper Bridge on the Big Deschutes to reach the grazing area. They placed salt blocks on the higher and dryer ground so the cattle would come up there and eat bunch grass. Otherwise, the cattle might stay by the river and eat only turf grass. Grace remembers how much fun it was to go to the ranges to check the cattle and bring them salt. The family would sometimes bring lunch along and take their time.

The Army took over the Spring River grazing area in December 1942 when Camp Abbot was being built in the Sunriver area. The Vandeverts summered their cattle at Sparks Lake up in the Cascades the following summer. Facing the loss of the nearby summer range at Spring River, good prices for beef, and the desire to help the war effort, the family sold all their cattle in the summer of 1943. They bought new cattle to restock the ranch after the war was over.

For winter feeding, Claude Senior and Uncle Bill grew rye in the big meadows above the Homestead. This was rye grain, like that used to make rye whisky, not rye grass. The children sometimes nibbled on the grain in the field. Grace remembers, "Before we took the cattle to range in the spring, Dad (Claude Senior) and Claude (Claude Junior, Grace's older brother) would plant the two rye fields. Depending on how hard the ground was, we would run the plow to cut the soil up. Then we would disk it, harrow it (break up clods and level the ground by dragging disks with spiny teeth through the soil), plant the seed by throwing it from a tub in the back of a wagon, cover it up, and wait and pray for rain."

Mowing rye at the ranch.

The amount of rye harvested depended almost entirely on how much rain there was in the spring and early summer. It might have been cost-effective to run a pump for irrigation from the river, but all the water in the river was allocated to farmers further downstream. In August 1926, Pearl Vandevert, Grace's mother, wrote her Aunt Linnie,

> "We haven't had any rain since May and maybe before as I can't remember when it did rain last.... You ask about our crops? They are so poor that it was hardly worthwhile to cut it. They got four loads (of hay) off of this place to 63 loads last year.... We had a freeze the 17th of June that killed everything.... They can't irrigate this place so had to watch everything dry up. We have enough hay here for the milk cows this winter, but the boys have started to look for hay to buy already. Two years ago, they paid out $1,700 for hay, but I hope not this year. They have about 220 cattle, counting calves, but they want to sell at least 100 head this fall."

Grace remembers,

> "The crop would be ready in the latter part of July. Dad took the mower pulled by the team of horses and cut the rye. Then Claude would come along with the rake, also pulled by horses, and get the rye

> into shocks along rows that were far enough apart to bring the hay wagon alongside. Dad would pitch the hay into the wagon. Claude would pile it onto the slings that would later lift the hay into the barn. It would take about an hour to get one load of hay. Claude would unhitch the horses and take them around to the back of the barn and hitch them to the pull-up ropes. Dad would attach the ropes to the slings of hay in the wagon, and then Claude would have the team pull the load up and into the barn. The whole job of getting a good crop in took about two to three weeks. We made homemade root beer in the summer, and I would bring it to them in the afternoon.
>
> "I remember the haying so well because one year I helped my Dad do everything except the raking. Claude was working for the Forest Service that year as a lookout east of Paulina Peak. It was during World War II when Camp Abbot was in operation. Soldiers on maneuvers camped outside the ranch and hung over the fence to watch us. I'm sure we looked very dusty and dirty. But so did they!"

The barn where the hay was stored was just south of a lone ponderosa that is still there today about halfway up the hill from the Homestead. The barn faced west toward the river and there were sheds up against the north and south sides. The sheds were about 10 feet high, 15 feet wide, and 50 feet long from front to back with wide doors at both ends. The north shed was for milking and the south shed for storing saddles and harnesses. Horses came into the shed to be harnessed and were tied to a railing that ran the whole length of the barn. There was a small shed for shearing sheep at the west end of the horse shed and a small pen off the cow shed for calves to stay in. No animals stayed in the barn or the sheds overnight unless they were very sick.

There were windows in the loft that were used to throw the hay down to the ground where it was put into shocks for the cattle in the winter. It was an efficient system because it was easy to throw the hay over the sheds or out the front over the sheep-shearing section. If the weather got very cold, the cattle would get two feedings a day, but they always stayed outside. Claude Junior says, "They were okay as long as their bellies were full."

Sometimes Claude Senior would heat half a barrel of sorghum

molasses and pour it on the shocks to give the cattle extra nourishment. "The bonfire was nice to get close to," remembers Grace. "It was darned cold."

Grace says, "I don't think we ever had to herd the cattle on the ranch. They knew the routine and they simply followed it. They got fed twice a day at the barn in the wintertime and they were ready for it. Then they would wander the pastures and eat or lie down during the day."

The cattle were generally free of disease. In years when blackleg appeared in the area, the cattle were vaccinated for it. Blackleg affects young cattle, killing them within 12 to 48 hours after the first appearance of symptoms. Fortunately, vaccination is very effective, requiring the injection of a capsule three-fourths of an inch long and one-fourth of an inch in diameter. The capsule is placed in hypodermic barrel with a plunger, called a gun, and the gun is shoved under the skin in the cattle's neck area. The ranch never lost any cattle to blackleg.

Bill Vandevert imported the Hashknife brand he knew well from Texas and Arizona. The brand originated in Weatherford, Texas, in the 1870s. The design was taken from the knives used by cattle camp cooks to cut beef and vegetables into cubes to make hash. The blade was a 180° curve with tails on the ends of it. A straight shaft connected the back of the blade in the middle of the curve to a handle so the cook could rock the blade back and forth easily. The key advantage of the Hashknife brand was that it was difficult for rustlers to superimpose another brand on top of it.

Aztec, the company Bill worked for in Arizona, put the brand, with

The Hashknife Brand.

the blade pointing up, on both sides of the animal's ribcage and sometimes on the left hip as well. Branding on both sides of the ribcage made for more work at branding time, but Aztec seemed to feel this would help deter rustlers. With the vast lands and spread-out herds, rustling was a popular occupation in Northern Arizona. One outlaw, who obviously did not have a heart for the cattle, cut the brand off entirely and sewed the skin back together.

Grace's brother Claude says, "Our brand was on the left side about midway between the front and back legs. Also, I think one ear of each heifer (female yearling) was underbitted, simply to make it easier to identify them when separating them from the steers."

The Hashknife name and brand still appear in a variety of locations around Vandevert Ranch today, most prominently in Hashknife Road, which bridges the Little Deschutes River and serves most of the houses.

Grace remembers,

> "Branding was done at both the Homestead ranch and Uncle Bill's ranch at Paulina Prairie. The calves were born from February until as late as May 15. The early ones were branded and castrated once they were a month old. But most of the calves would go to the range with their mothers and be branded in the fall when they returned.
>
> "The branding was done in a log corral with three or four men to handle the cattle. The corral was good sized, about 50 feet from the barn, with a fence from the pasture for the cattle to come in and exit back to the field.
>
> "There was a fire burning in the middle of the corral and the branding irons—usually two of them—were red hot when heated. One man would rope a yearling, pull it down on its side, and apply the brand. Then the animal was let up, checked, and released into the field. Dad told me it didn't hurt the cattle to be branded and they only bawled because they were tied down. I think they felt it but they seemed to recover quickly. Male calves were castrated at that same time and were watched carefully to see that they healed okay. They usually just returned to their mothers and were fine.
>
> "The cattle were branded just once in their lifetime. Hair would

grow into the brand but would fall off in the spring."

Nita Lowry, author of *The Triangle Outfit* about the Stearns Cattle Company, wrote in a letter to Grace, "In the 1950s, one of the Stearns purebred cows had twin calves when they trailed from La Pine to the Crooked River Ranch. She wintered there and when it came time to brand the calves the crew looked over the cow and saw your Dad's brand on her. She had horns, was a Hereford, and with her long winter hair they had failed to see she wasn't a Stearns cow. Harry Stearns promptly took her and the calves back to Claude. He was pleased. He told Harry that was pretty good—got his cow wintered and two big calves in the bargain." The former Stearns ranch in La Pine is now owned by one of the current residents of Vandevert Ranch.

There was generally one milking cow to supply the family, giving four to five gallons of milk per milking with two milkings a day. The cream was skimmed off and either made into butter for the family or sold to the dairy store in Bend. The store picked the cream up at the mailbox on Highway 97. There were stanchions in the shed to put the cows into while they were milked. The milk was not pasteurized but the Vandeverts were very careful about keeping the cows and the milking area clean. It would be impossible to sell that unpasteurized milk today, but the lumber camps were happy to have it. The Vandeverts themselves were drinking it and it never made them sick.

There was also a milking corral across the river from the house and a fenced-in pasture beyond it that went all the way west to the property line. The cows with calves stayed in one or the other at night for their protection. The family milked a cow in that area only occasionally. When the river flooded in the spring, however, the only way to get across the river and milk a cow was to row a boat that was kept tied to the back porch.

The small milk house or cool house was just north of the Homestead kitchen where it was in the shade much of the day. The walls and doors were packed with eight inches of sawdust for insulation. In the summer, the family could keep the temperature in the milk house below 50 degrees (but not as cold as a refrigerator) by opening the door at night and closing it during the day. There was a screen door to keep varmints out. The milk house was also good for keeping milk from freezing in the winter.

"I don't know why I have always had a soft spot for that old butter churn," says Grace. "It was just something that we used regularly and then stored bread in.

"When we made butter, we brought the churn into the kitchen and sat it on a little wooden stand so that we could turn it end-over-end with the handle that attached about half-way down the outside of the barrel. We put the cream into the churn and sealed the lid tight with a special fixture on top shaped like a propeller. It took about 30 to 45 minutes to get the cream to turn to butter and we took turns. Dad was at the house for lunch for a couple of hours due to the timing of ranch work and my Mother would have him do it then. We churned every two to three weeks and got from three to six pounds of butter each time. There was a wooden plug in the top to let the liquid drain out. This was usually very good buttermilk.

Vandevert butter churn—now at the Des Chutes Historical Museum.

"Then, Dad took the butter and put it into a wooden bowl and worked the butter back and forth with a wooden spatula to get all the extra liquid out. Once that was done, he made it into cubes that we wrapped in special paper and put in a crock in the milk house, set in cool water to keep it fresh.

"When we were done with all that, we cleaned the churn thoroughly and took it back into the pantry. We used the churn every day to put my Mother's home-made bread in. The churn had a tight seal and the bread kept better inside it."

Bill Vandevert sold his cattle one at a time to neighbors or to people who were passing through. The family never butchered cattle just for themselves because they had no way to keep even half a steer from spoiling before they consumed it. In the early days, area ranchers would take turns butchering cattle and sharing the beef with each other. Later, when the butcher in Bend asked for a beef the family would slaughter one and take the meat to him. The family would keep some of the beef or have the butcher send back some of the best steaks. A letter from Bill Vandevert's daughter-in-law Pearl in 1935 recounts one time the family kept part of an animal they butchered. "We butchered about 10 days before Christmas so Claude and I canned 25½ pints of beef and 38 pints of vegetable soup. It took four days, and I was too tired to do anything else. I was so tickled to get it finished as the meat and soup came in so handy."

The family ate better-tasting beef than is generally available in grocery stores today. It was largely grass fed, rather than being fattened on corn and other grains. The beef grew to full size more slowly and was led to slaughter when it was two years old, as opposed to about one year in the feed lots of today. Grace says,

> "Beef was always the most flavorful of all the meats that we ate. We had to either can it in jars or cut it up and take it to freezer space in Bend. We gave some away to family or neighbors. It had to be taken care of quickly due to spoilage with no refrigeration.
>
> "My Mother made hash, meat pie, beef and noodles, beef stews, and we always had hamburger from the freezer in Bend. There were numerous ways to cook beef in those days and we used most of them. We didn't need anything except salt and pepper—and very little of that. We had beef most of the year-round.
>
> "I'd give anything to have one of Dad's steaks fried on that Home Comfort stove in the kitchen at the ranch again. There has never been a better steak cooked that I can remember. Today, I'm totally concerned where I buy beef of any kind. I have to know the place it came from or the butcher. I'm such a pain!"

Bill may have sold some cattle to Sid Stearns. But it became more practical to market cattle to the larger economy when the railroad came to Bend in 1911. The Vandeverts gathered the steers and culled some of the cows in the fall and sent at least fifty cattle to Portland. A railroad car held 50 head and sometimes the brothers sent two cars.

Prior to 1928, the men herded the cattle to the railroad in Bend the day before they were to be shipped. It was a long day's ride. After 1928, when the rail line between Bend and Chemult was completed, they herded the cattle to a siding near Paulina Prairie. They called the railroad in advance and the company left the cars they asked for on the siding. It was always a problem to truck in food and water for the cattle to consume overnight.

The cattle lost weight getting to the railroad and on the long trip to Portland. But the shrinkage was worth it because the prices in Portland were better than the local prices. One or both of the brothers went with the cattle to sell them at the Portland stockyards. In the better times, Claude Senior would stay one night at the Heathman, the best hotel in Portland.

The stockyard auctioned off the steers in lots of about 15 animals, with steers of similar quality in each lot. The cows were auctioned separately. The cattle with the Hashknife brand were referred to as "range-fattened" and "graded" cattle, but there was no formal grading system.

It was a struggle for the family to keep the cattle business as profitable as it was in the early teens due to nationwide trends and to particular happenstance. In his book *Prime Cut*, Jimmy Skaggs writes: "When measured by parity—that is when their income is compared with the generally prosperous period 1910–1914, relative to prices paid by the agrarian community for all goods and services, including interest—farmers and ranchers lost 18 percent to a ratcheting economy between 1920 and 1929, and another 44 percent following the crash (of 1929), reaching the bottom of the abyss in 1932. Ten years later (1942)...the typical farmer netted only 105 percent of parity."

The Depression in the 1930s was very tough on everyone, bur livestock farmers like the Vandeverts generally did a little better than crop farmers. The family was never hungry because they had their own sheep, chickens, and eggs to sell and to eat. The drought that caused the Dust Bowl in the middle of the country did not hit the upriver area where the ranch was. Grace remembers a happy childhood. Claude Junior says, "We were poor, but we didn't know it."

One cattle transaction cost the ranch dearly for years. Claude Senior was called into the Army when the United States entered World War I in 1917. He was 25 years old and not yet married. Armistice was declared before he went overseas and Claude returned to the ranch in 1918. In the meantime, his older brother Bill, 31 at the time, had to manage all the ranches and all the cattle.

A local banker came to Uncle Bill and asked him to take 100 head of cattle that the bank had acquired in a foreclosure. Bill said he did not want the cattle, but the banker offered him a good price and encouraged him to take them to help provide meat for the soldiers. Bill finally agreed, but said he was much too busy to handle them right away and the bank would have to pasture and feed them over the summer. The cattle were on the other side of Bend and Bill could not even spare enough time to go look at them.

When Uncle Bill went to pick up the cattle in the fall, there were only 12 head left out of 100. Bill could not sell the cattle for anywhere near the cost of the 100 cattle he had bought. He took out a loan from the same bank to make up the difference. When Claude came back from the war, he found that the two ranches were almost bankrupt.

The repercussions of the missing cattle rippled through the Vandevert family history for a full generation. Claude Junior reports, "Dad paid on that loan all through the Depression. The family would have gotten through the Depression okay, except for the debt to the bank. Every fall, Dad would sell cattle, pay the interest on the loan, pay the grocery bill, and pay the taxes. Then he was broke." The family sold milk, butter, and eggs and the younger Claude cut wood and did odd jobs just to get some cash for the family. Sometimes his father could make four dollars a day hiring himself out with two horses to do "Fresno work" on the Dalles-California Highway. This was before the widespread use of bulldozers and earth movers. Claude and his team moved dirt and rocks using a patented Fresno Scraper.

Claude Junior reports that some of the principal on the loan was paid in the 1920s when times were better. But during the Depression, the price of live beef was only $2.00 per hundredweight and all the family could pay was the interest. When the price of beef went up in 1938, it had a dramatic effect on the family. They finally paid off the loan completely. In 1941, the family bought its first good car, an almost new 1941 two-door Chevrolet sedan that someone had traded in. The elder Claude loved the fact that his wife finally got to ride in a nice car. He drove his two daughters, Grace and Mary Jean, over to the Willamette Valley to pick fruit. They thought that was quite a treat.

The banker had entrusted the herd to his brother-in-law who may have sold most of it over the summer and pocketed the money. Much later, in the 1950s, the banker told the Vandeverts that if they had gotten a lawyer they could have broken the bank.

Claude Senior sold off the last of the cattle in 1971, a year after he sold the ranch to Leonard Lundgren with the condition that Claude and his wife could continue to live there. While cattle dominated the ranch for almost 80 years, they shared it with many other animals kept by the Vandeverts. There will be more about the other animals in a later chapter.

CHAPTER 6

Community

Bend had a population of 21 in 1900, only a dozen more people than Vandevert Ranch. Bend started to grow when irrigation from the Deschutes River made farming viable. Alexander Drake established the first major irrigation system, the Pilot Butte Development Company, and water started flowing in 1904. Bend incorporated as a city in December of that year.

In January 1905, Bend welcomed its first licensed doctor, Urling Coe. He later became mayor of Bend and was the city's first banker. Dr .Coe wrote a highly entertaining history of his time in Bend called *Frontier Doctor*. He was attracted to what he saw as, "the largest area in the United States without a railroad and the last frontier of the thrilling and romantic Old West." He was not disappointed. Three days after his arrival, a bear visited the town by swimming across the Deschutes River. Bend's first year as a city was marked by a typhoid epidemic. Dr. Coe persuaded the population to clean up the sewers to stop the spread of the disease and taught people to improve the health of the citizenry. Dr. Coe served the citizens of Bend for 13 years.

Drake, the irrigation pioneer, was farsighted enough to realize Bend's biggest opportunity lay in the timber west and south of the city. He laid out the town with space for two large sawmills. Then Bend anxiously awaited the arrival of the railroad so it would have a way to get the lumber to markets. The economic opportunity was so great it gave rise to the last railroad-building race in the West.

Two famous railroad men, Edward Harriman and Jim Hill, started their respective railroads south from the Columbia River at about the same time: Harriman building up the east bank of the Deschutes and Hill building up the west but crossing over north of where the Crooked River flowed into the Deschutes from the east. The track-laying projects were among the very last done with picks, shovels, and wheelbarrows rather than heavy equipment. The race was finally decided by a court that ruled Jim Hill would build and own the final leg of the railroad to Bend, but Harriman would have the right to use it. Hill got the upper hand by buying land surrounding the only practical place to cross the Crooked River.

The Crooked River railroad bridge ninety-nine years after construction.

Crossing the gorge of the Crooked River was the biggest construction challenge in building the railroad. The bridge, built from both sides of the gorge, was a noted engineering marvel in its day and is still one of the highest railroad bridges in the nation. Grace says, "My mother's brothers and her father worked on the Crooked River Bridge. They came from Portland and pitched a tent and lived there through the summers until it was done."

The railroad finally reached Bend on "Railroad Day," October 5, 1911. Jim Hill came to Bend to drive the final spike. The railroad changed Bend forever. "The old frontier went with the golden spike," said Dr. Coe. Bend's population grew 10-fold between 1910 and 1920.

Though there were smaller lumber companies earlier, the two companies that drove the growth of Bend for 40 years built their first mills

Pearl Catlow Vandevert with her three brothers who worked on the Crooked River railroad bridge for Jim Hill.

in 1916. The Brooks-Scanlon mill was on the east bank of the Deschutes and the Shevlin-Hixon mill was on the west. Brooks-Scanlon built a second, larger mill a short distance upriver in 1922. In time, the three mills would turn out more than 500 million board feet of lumber a year and be among the largest sawmills in the world. They sometimes ran around the clock and had over 4,000 employees.

Bend and the surrounding area experienced a real estate boom. The leading Bend booster, William D. Cheney, was especially interested in attracting citizens and investment from Seattle. A "Bend-Seattle Banquet" on September 2, 1912, featured veal from Vandevert Ranch and a talk on the local climate by Dr. Coe, president of the First National Bank. As he wrote, "The marked absence of infection in that country was always a marvel to me and I never ceased to wonder at it.... It was probably owing to the fact that the air was so pure and dry, and there was so much sunshine."

Bill Vandevert, refusing to acknowledge there was any job he could not do, had already been in the real estate business for years. He had been cutting hay at Crane Prairie when the Forest Homestead Act of 1906 made it seem the prairie might open up to homesteading. The *Bend Bulletin* of July 29, 1906, reported that Bill was locating homesteaders on the land and getting them to send their applications to Washington. But Crane Prairie did not meet the provisions of the law and the few who tried to homestead on the land were evicted. In 1922, the Deschutes River was dammed to turn Crane Prairie into a reservoir.

By 1913, Bill Vandevert was vice president of the Oregon Investment Company in Bend. The president was Elmer Niswonger. The company covered the gamut of improved and unimproved real estate, town property, homestead land, timber lands, money to loan, and even "sick, accident, and life insurance." Bill had earlier owned land where people expected the railroad station to be built. He swapped for 80 acres near Eighth Street and Greenwood.

Bill Vandevert was the deputy sheriff for the "upriver country" around the ranch when it was part of Crook County and, after 1916, when Deschutes County split from Crook County. Bill was bailiff of the Deschutes County circuit court in Bend from 1917 to 1937. He was an active member of the Bend Commercial Club, the Masons, and the Pioneer Association.

Bill Vandevert's Deputy Sheriff Badge.

Sometime in these early years, a quarrelsome family named Donkel settled in the upriver area. The mother of the family died mysteriously and the father disappeared. Bill assisted in the search for the father. The man's body was found buried under a smoldering fire. He had been shot in the back of the head and the bullet had lodged against his temple. A member of the search party said it looked like the man had been shot with a .45 pistol. Bill had the only .45 pistol around and insisted the bullet be dug out. The local doctor tried sawing through the skull, but he did not have his surgeon's tools with him. He gave up in disgust. Bill was determined to remove any doubt in anyone's mind and he sawed the dead man's head open. The sheriff picked up a table fork and dug out the bullet—a .32 caliber slug.

While the Vandeverts lived on their ranch for almost 100 years, the families around them came and went. Big Meadow, between the Deschutes River and the future site of Sunriver Lodge, was sold in 1904 for $2,300 by James Pelton to Fred A. Shonquest, and the land was called "Shonquest Meadow" for many years. A couple named Atkinson bought land next to the Shonquests and became active in the local community. John Atkinson was an Englishman and a world traveler, and his wife was Hawaiian. Though the couple had no children, Mr. Atkinson began serving on the local school board in 1915. Anzonetta Caldwell Rupe, who was a child in the 1920s, wrote, "Mr. Atkinson had a beautiful 1916 Model T with no top and a brass radiator, carriage lamps, and a horn that squawked loudly when someone squeezed the rubber bulb. We all loved his car, especially the horn. Mr. Atkinson took us for a ride in it one day—a treat I have never forgotten."

By the time Grace was growing up in the 1930s, the Atkinsons had been replaced by a family named Fox. "The house and outbuildings were approximately where the Sunriver Lodge is now. I don't know if they ran cattle in the meadows or whether they even owned the property. It may have been part of or maybe all of the property owned by the family of Sid Stearns, the cattleman."

Just north of Vandevert Ranch, where the Crosswater Golf Course is today, the Allens owned a sheep ranch. Court Allen and his sister

July 4 picnic at the Big Meadows School in about 1897. Front row left to right, Maude and Clint Vandevert, Eva West, Kathryn Grace Vandevert, Carrie Fee (teacher), Claude Vandevert Senior, Madie Aldrich. Second row Goldie West, Mrs. Glen Slack (teacher), Leona Aldrich, Uncle Bill and George Vandevert. Carrie Fee's father was a judge on the federal Court of Appeals for the Ninth Circuit.

are buried in a small cemetery just west of the 11th fairway. The cemetery is considered "ground under repair" and golfers get a free drop. A family named Elliot began renting the ranch in 1921. Over 80 years later in 2007, Mildred Elliot West wrote to Grace, "My sister and I had happy memories of summers we spent on the Little Deschutes." There are photos in the Crosswater Clubhouse of dipping and counting sheep on that ranch and one photo of Mildred's sister, Mable Elliott, holding a string of trout caught in the river.

When Grace was a child, the Allen ranch belonged to the Dalys. "Their three children went to school at Harper corner and on our ranch when the school was moved there. I think they had both sheep and cattle. The Dalys moved into Bend in the mid-1930s. My Mother and I visited with Mrs. Daly at their home there. Her daughter and I stayed friends in later years until she passed away. She and her mother were at the ranch the day I was born and she loved to tell me about it."

The records Grace uncovered for School District 34 show how sporadic school was and how many familiar names appear among the teachers and the school board directors.

Register of Teachers Employed in School District No. 34: Big Meadow

Teacher	Director(s)	Monthly Salary	Commencing School	Term (Weeks)
Emma Buchanan	J. Whitfield D. C. Brownell C. B. Allen	$35	Apr. 24, 1899	14
S. Clarke	W. P. Vandevert	$35	Dec. 4, 1899	18
Lily Knox	Dick Vandevert*	$35	Jan. 4, 1901	18
Jessie Andrews	S. D. Donkel W. P. Vandevert	$40	Feb. 26, 1903	12
Elva J. Smith	C. B. Allen	$45	May 3, 1904	12
Maude Vandevert	J. E. Ryan	$45	Jun. 25, 1905	6
Mrs. Frank Minor	C. B. Allen, George Bates	$50	Oct. 6, 1908	16
Kathryn Grace Vandevert	Charles M. Kirkbride J. E. Sawhill F. Shonquist	$60	Nov. 15, 1909	12
Kathryn Grace Vandevert	Same as above	$60	Feb. 12, 1910	12
Carolyn Heyburn	Same as above	$60	Sep. 26, 1910	12
E. Meriam Allen	Same as above	$60	Mar. 14, 1911	12
Adelaide Teogome (*sp?*)	Same as above	$60	May 6, 1912	24
Adelaide Teogome (*sp?*)	M. J. Main C. B. Allen	$70	Oct. 21, 1912	24
Katherine Demply	C. B. Allen M. J. Miller	$70	Dec. 1, 1913	24
Emma Roberts	Same as above	$70	Sep. 28, 1914	12
Emma Roberts	Same as above	$70	Jan. 4, 1915	20
Bertha Ransom	C. B. Allen, John Atkinson	$70	Dec. 6, 1915	24
Frederick L. Rice	Same as above	$65	Oct. 9, 1916	24

* Dick Vandevert was William Plutarch Vandevert's brother. He ran a stagecoach service between Silver Lake and Bend. Another director signed with him whose name is difficult to read, something similar to F.C. Imanhue.

CHAPTER 7

Ranchers

The two brothers who decided to make a life of ranching and cattle were Thomas William, known as "Uncle Bill," and Claude, known in this book as "Claude Senior" because he had a son named Claude Chandler Vandevert Junior.

The *La Pine Intermountain* newspaper of July 7, 1921 reported that the brothers won two races at the Third Annual La Pine "Waumpoo." Uncle Bill, giving an early indication of his career with horses, won the "Free-for-All" on a horse named Mable. The newspaper said that Mable posed as an ordinary work horse during the year but always seemed to win a prize ribbon or two on July 4. Claude Senior won the 100-yard dash, narrowly defeating Cecil Hollinshead. Many years later Claude's son David ran track for Bend High School and received a track scholarship from Linfield College.

Uncle Bill (1884–1969) was Bill and Sadie's oldest son and second-oldest child. He loved telling the story of the time his parents moved the family from his grandfather's ranch in Powell Butte to their new home on the Little Deschutes. The first night they camped on the Big Deschutes near what was then called Farewell Bend. They came to the ranch on the second day. Uncle Bill, then eight years old, led the milk cow all the way. The cow was essential for a family with six children. Uncle Bill thought he had done a good job. He turned 18 in 1902, seven years before Bend High School had its first graduating class, and he finished high school at Willamette University in Salem.

At one point, Uncle Bill started to build a log cabin on land just west of the ranch but abandoned it. The developers of the modern ranch acquired that land in the late 1980s and the remains of Uncle Bill's half-built cabin can still be found today in the west woodlands.

Uncle Bill's cabin was never finished. It sat on land adjacent to the ranch that the modern developers added in the late 1980's.

In 1913 or 1914, Uncle Bill bought a 360-acre ranch at Paulina Prairie, on the east side of Huntington Road. The ranch had an advantage over the original Vandevert Homestead in that it was irrigated by a ditch that ran down the middle of it. The ranch had a two-story, three-bedroom house and a large barn to the east with a few sheds for poultry. The buildings are gone today, but the land now belongs to a retired aerospace engineer and his wife who named the ranch "Leaning Pine" and have a long waiting list for their grass-fed beef.

Uncle Bill socialized with a series of young women before he finally married at age 42. In 1927, he married Dorothy Belle Brasel, a member of the Catlow family, in Portland. The couple had one daughter, Barbara, who was five months older than Grace. Grace and Barbara were first cousins through their fathers and third cousins through their mothers. They were great friends.

The well behind the Paulina Prairie house sometimes went dry and the water was not good for drinking or for washing clothes. Dorothy and her daughter came to the Homestead every week to do the laundry. Not only did the Homestead have better water, it had a gasoline-powered washing machine. Laundry day provided a good chance for

Dorothy to visit her second cousin Pearl and for Barbara to play with Grace.

Dorothy's bachelor brother, Johnny Brasel, lived with the couple at Paulina Prairie. Johnny built a log playhouse for Barbara that she enjoyed with her cousins from the Homestead for many hours. The children were not supposed to play with what they called bullfrogs under the main house, but the huge frogs, or toads, were very intriguing.

Barbara and Dorothy Vandevert, Uncle Bill's family.

In the summers, when Claude and Bill's brother Arthur visited from Kentucky for a month, Uncle Bill, Claude, and Arthur would take their children on a two-night camping trip—usually to Cultus Lake in the Cascades. Bill would be in charge of making biscuits at breakfast and dinner. He could cook anything the party needed with his Dutch-oven pot.

Uncle Bill worked from sunup to sundown. When he moved his family to Tumalo in 1935, Bill started working with racehorses. He raised them, trained them, and took them throughout Oregon, California, and Washington to run. He would always take them to the ocean to run in the salt water as it was good for their hooves. Later the family moved east of Pilot Butte and had a strawberry farm. Dorothy started working at St. Charles Hospital when it was still in downtown Bend. The couple's last home was in Bend on 13th Street where they could relax with a modern home and many friends coming and going. Dorothy was a wonderful seamstress. She sewed gowns for dolls of the First Ladies of the United States to match the dresses they wore to the inaugural balls. She took great delight in tracking down and using the same material that had been in the original gowns. Her dolls were donated to the Des Chutes Historical Museum. Uncle Bill died in 1969 and Dorothy in 1984.

Claude Senior was born on January 6, 1892, at his grandfather's ranch in Powell Butte, just before his parents began homesteading Vandevert Ranch. He attended the local schools and graduated from Bend High School in 1910 when he was 18.

Claude's daughter, Mary Jean, wrote, "My father, Claude Chandler Vandevert Senior, had the most integrity and was the most honorable and honest person I knew, along with all his many other wonderful traits."

Sometime before October 1913, Claude went to Portland to work for the North West Electric Company. He sometimes worked seven days a week, and, for recreation, he boxed with his Chief Operator. He said the man was very good at it.

A few months later, the company sent him to Underwood, Washington—across the Columbia River from Hood River, Oregon. Claude worked as an "oiler" and made $75.00 a month. He paid $22.50 for room and board and liked the area better than Portland. It was a rural area more like what he was used to on the ranch. But his letters to his sister Kathryn Grace revealed how lonesome he was for the family. He liked his boss but was bothered that the man cursed around his own little girls. Claude wrote that he was reading *Les Miserables* and did not think it would take him long to finish it because it was so interesting.

When a family member had to go to Portland from the ranch, they would go by way of The Dalles and cross the river to visit Claude. Claude Senior kept thinking of the ranch but wanted to stick with his job. In the next year or so, he was transferred back to Portland to be groomed for advancement. It seemed the company liked his work very much. He returned to Underwood briefly, but he finally decided to leave the company and come back to the ranch.

The principal reason Claude returned was that he loved the ranch and enjoyed ranch life. Another may have been that in 1914 raising cattle on the ranch looked like a good way to make a living. The Bend area and the cattle business were both thriving. Claude's parents undoubtedly were glad to have him home for his company and to help them manage the ranch. Claude's father Bill was 60 years old in 1914 and was surely finding he could not do as much as he used to.

Claude Senior counted himself lucky that he was able to live on the ranch virtually his whole life. But he sometimes wondered if he would have been financially better off had he stayed with the electric company. The men he started with all rose to become executives.

Claude knew members of the Catlow family in Portland because his older sister, Maude, had married Chester Catlow in 1912. About that same time, Chet's uncle, Dan Catlow, moved his family to Oregon from Atlantic, Iowa. They brought with them four sons and their beautiful 12-year-old daughter, Pearl Marie Catlow, born on June 24, 1900. Pearl was later to become the heart and soul of Vandevert Ranch.

The Vandeverts and the extended Catlow family came to be close friends, and the Vandeverts stayed with the Catlows when they were in Portland. Claude undoubtedly met Pearl when she was still in high school, but romance did not blossom until she was a few years older.

Pearl held several jobs after graduating from high school. One required using a "comptomerator machine" for entering data. The machine looked like a big old mechanical calculator. One might say she worked in the information technology industry before there was an information technology industry.

Pearl Catlow Vandevert, mother of the author.

On October 15, 1922, when Pearl was 22, she married Claude in Portland. People said that Claude and Pearl were the most in love couple they ever knew. Certainly Pearl must have loved Claude to leave behind her civilized life in Portland. She moved across the Cascades to Vandevert Ranch and became the lady of the house. Pearl could ride a horse, ice skate on the river, swim, drive a car, and sew dresses for her girls and patches for her men. She was a fun-loving mother, wife, and daughter-in-law. She was even the secretary for what was then School District 25 at Harper.

Claude's mother Sadie was having health problems and stayed in Bend to be near doctors. She died in 1924, two years after Pearl came to the Homestead. Pearl took over the running of the five-bedroom log home and all the meals and work that went with it. She ran the house with no running water, no electricity, a wood stove to cook on, and few of the comforts she was used to at her family's home. Grace says her mother did everything with a charm and kindness that made the ranch a very happy place.

The Homestead was very active in the 1920s and 1930s. It had been, and still was, a stop-over for people traveling from The Dalles to California and back. Due to the scarcity of lodging in the area at that time, Sadie and then Pearl took on the responsibility of putting up travelers. Anyone stopping by would always find a bite to eat and a place to rest. Pearl wrote her aunt in Iowa about how 12 people came by in wagons on the way south and she fed them, bedded them down and saw that their horses were cared for. She made $19.00 for that one time and felt very good about it.

Pearl entered into all aspects of ranch life. She drove the horses while Claude sowed grain from the back of the wagon every spring. She could help bring in the wood, carry water when needed, make three meals a day from scratch, wash several loads of clothes with the gas-driven washing machine, and, the next day, iron the clothes with a heavy iron heated on the wood stove. She seemed to manage everything without effort.

When Pearl and Claude heard that the Army would build a training camp nearby they had the idea to buy a couple of the barracks after World War II and move the buildings to the ranch to establish a children's camp. Claude Senior always wanted to call it "Indian Meadows."

Pearl and Claude had five children: Claude Junior (born 1923), Danny (1927), Grace (1929), Mary Jean (1934), and David (1942).

When Grace reconnected with her mother's family in Iowa and visited them in 2007, they had a surprise for her—a box of letters from Pearl and Pearl's brother Charlie to their Aunt Linnie. The family had kept the letters for over 70 years. Excerpts from Pearl's letters appear

Claude Senior and Pearl with three of their children—
Grace, Mary Jean, and Claude Junior.

throughout this book. But the saddest letter she wrote was certainly one from 1930 about the death of her son Danny at the age of three:

"Someday I would like to know why our loved ones have to be taken from us. Danny...was never sick and the best little fellow I ever saw.... I suppose you heard that he stepped on a nail on a Saturday and the next Saturday he was gone. We didn't know a thing was wrong till Friday noon when he had convulsions. Of course Arthur, a doctor, was here and he was with him all the time. But the medicine they gave him I guess was too much for his heart. George and Clint (Claude's other doctor brothers) were also with him and George was with him all Friday night, also Arthur, but I guess we just had to lose him. It was so hard on the boys as they can save others but they couldn't save him. But it was the first case they ever had of tetanus and the first case that had ever been in Bend. It is very rare out west here. In old countries, it is much worse.

"It was very hard on Claude as Danny was such a daddy's boy. The day he stepped on the nail, Claude took him to the circus and he had such a wonderful time. Some thought we didn't watch his foot, but not five minutes after he stepped on the nail Arthur had tended to it and George dressed it again that afternoon. Then Arthur tended to it every day."

A vaccine for tetanus had been invented in 1924 but was not widely used until World War II.

The ranch was the favorite gathering place for the extended family. Pearl organized and cooked many Thanksgiving and Christmas dinners, sometimes for almost two dozen people. Grace and Claude Junior remember the Christmases of the 1930s fondly.

"Christmas brought the wider family together at the Old Homestead. It was quite a strain on our Mother, but she always looked forward to it and wanted it to happen. She liked lots of company and so did Dad.

"In 1934, however, our mother had higher priorities than her guests. Our sister, Mary Jean, was born on the ranch the afternoon of December 24th. Our mother was in her bed at the south end of the downstairs. Christmas Eve was held in the living room, just across a hallway, so she could almost feel part of the group. Even though there had been a birth, there was still a house full of people. At least Mom didn't have to provide meals for them. That year they cooked for her.

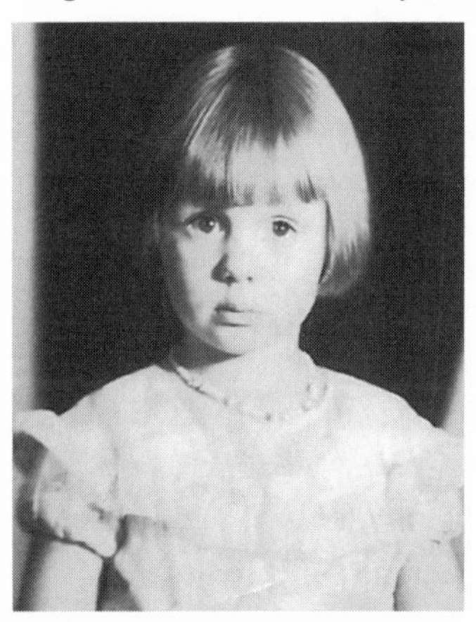

Grace Vandevert McNellis as a child.

"Grace was only five years old that year. We went down to school that day and when we got home in the afternoon, there was a baby sister. Grace was thrilled with her and thought she was her Christmas doll. Mary Jean was a redhead and very cute.

"Our folks had little to purchase presents. They were usually very practical presents like clothing and such, but usually at least one thing that we really wanted. Christmas plans started in November when we would receive the Montgomery Ward's Christmas catalog. Everyone got a chance to go through the catalog and make notes of what they wanted. That didn't mean they would get what they picked out, but there was always a chance.

"When Mary Jean was old enough to walk, we went with our mother to J.C. Penney's store in Bend. All the toys were in two or three aisles in the basement. We would walk through and look at every one of them. Penney's would even let us try out the tricycles in the aisles.

"Meantime, Grace and her mother made gifts for the aunts, uncles, and cousins that lived away and mailed them off. They were embroidery works on pillowcases and tea towels and also my mother's wonderful fruitcakes. Dad raised several turkeys for the family and may have sold some to neighbors at Christmas. If Dad did, it was not a business. Maybe it helped pay for some of our presents.

"On the Sunday before Christmas, we cut the tree. The family would all go out. The tree was usually a lodgepole pine from just north of the rock pile at the entrance gate. Dad probably pruned up several trees during the year to make them look better for Christmas. Sometimes the family would drive up to the cattle's summer range, by Spring River, and go up a little higher in the hills to pick the tree. The tree was decorated with a boxful of ornaments that had been used for years. We had candles on our Christmas tree before we got electricity. We had to be very careful and not touch it. It was very beautiful.

"In the late afternoon of Christmas Eve, Uncle Bill and Aunt Dorothy arrived with our cousin Barbara from the Paulina Ranch. Aunt Maude's family came from the Shevlin Camp or La Pine with their daughter, Kathryn, who was older than we were (born 1918). Sometimes Kathryn's older siblings, Bill and Betty, also came on Christmas Eve or on Christmas day.

"Since the 24th was also our sister Mary Jean's birthday, we gathered in the kitchen for a light supper and Mary's birthday cake and presents. We made sure she had her special time even with Christmas on our minds. Then we retired to the living room where the family exchanged gifts.

"The children all received gifts such as jig-saw puzzles, card games, Monopoly, marbles, jacks, and many other fun things. Grace remembers receiving autograph books. But her favorite gift from those days was a Brownie Box Camera that her brother Claude gave her. She loved that camera and took many pictures over the years that we still have.

"We finished up about 10 o'clock and, in most cases, the visiting family stayed at the ranch overnight. The next morning, Uncle Bill and Johnny Brasel would go back to Paulina Ranch to milk the cows and take care of the chores before they returned. The kids rose early and ran to see what Santa Claus had left for them in the stockings by the old fireplace. Usually, a very special toy was there that had been yearned for in the catalog or the store and the rest was filled with nuts, candies, new toothbrushes, socks, and many other things.

"During the morning, the women shared the work of putting the Christmas dinner together. We all waited for Uncle Doc (Clint Vandevert) and Aunt Harriet, Joan, and Jack to arrive from Bend. Aunt Harriet brought more things for dinner. Then the men put the large table together in the dining room that would seat at least 20 people, and we sat down to the big turkey dinner with all the trimmings. In those days, we made everything from scratch because, with no refrigeration, we couldn't store things. It all worked beautifully and we sat there for well over an hour eating and enjoying every minute. Uncle Bill got his special pan of boiled parsnips that he loved.

"Grampa (William Plutarch Vandevert) sat at one end of the table. He must have taken great satisfaction celebrating Christmas in a house that he had built, on a ranch he had founded, surrounded by four of his eight children and many of his grandchildren. He talked and listened to everyone and then retired to the living room by the fireplace to continue with the men while the women cleaned up.

"Another special Christmas was either 1935 or 1936. About 4:00 p.m. on Christmas Eve, Dad and Claude Junior went to the barn to feed the cattle and milk the cow. It was snowing quite hard but we forgot about it and went ahead with the festivities. About 10:00 p.m. Dad's brother, Uncle Doc, said he thought he had better drive back to Bend and return for dinner the next day. He had just purchased a Chrysler Airflow. Well, when we went outside, there was two feet of fresh snow. No going home for anyone that night. So my Mother had to put up about 20 people, make breakfast the next morning, and provide lunch for them while Dad and Claude and the other men worked the better part of Christmas opening up the road to Highway 97 so everyone could go home. And can you believe it? Our mother always spoke of that time with great fondness."

CHAPTER 8

Timber

When the railroad reached Bend in 1911, it suddenly became economical to ship lumber to the outside world. Two lumber companies from Minnesota and Wisconsin had acquired thousands of acres of timberland around Bend earlier in the century. In 1915, Brooks-Scanlon built a mill on the east bank of the Deschutes and Shevlin-Hixon on the west bank. The demand for lumber was strong because of World War I.

Timber was expensive to move and the early industry attempted to move both logs and lumber by water whenever possible. Dean Hollinshead, a friend of the Vandevert family, got a job in 1917 floating lumber down the Little Deschutes from La Pine, where it had been milled, to just above Benham Falls on the Big Deschutes. He and two other men connected 42 rafts of lumber together with 2 x 12's and struggled with sandbars and the twists and turns of the river. They stuck a pole through a hole in the last raft so the last man could drag the pole along the bottom of the river to slow down the last raft and keep the flotilla from bunching up. The men learned how to handle the rafts as they went along, and when they reached the footbridge at Vandevert Ranch, they slipped the lumber easily beneath it. They thought they had the task pretty well in hand as they came downriver the second time. But they found Claude Vandevert Senior and two of his brothers standing on the footbridge looking rather stern. Some other rafters had walked on the riverbanks to push and pull their rafts and they had

Family guests on the footbridge about 1910. Obviously a good day for fishing.

trampled down the Vandevert's hay. Claude and his brothers wanted to make sure that did not happen again. Dean assured Claude he knew how to steer without getting out on land. His crew did a perfect job of guiding their lumber through the bridge. Then it was time to pull up the braking pole. The pole would not come. The top of the pole jammed on the bridge and pulled the entire bridge down, along with Claude and his brothers. Claude made a dive into the river that he and Dean talked about for years.

There were extensive forests all around Vandevert Ranch. In the late 1910s or early 1950s, Shevlin-Hixon paid the Vandeverts for the right to harvest some of the ponderosas on the eastern edge of the ranch.

If loggers could not move wood by water, the next best alternative was rail. Railroads handled more than half the timber operations in the Northwest until the 1950s. The railroads were gradually replaced with logging roads as Kenworth and other companies started building soft-tire trucks with powerful engines and strong brakes. Shevlin-Hixon built hundreds of miles of temporary railroads into the forest to retrieve logs and move them to the mill in Bend. The rail lines spread out across the forest like the branches of a tree. Once the crews had harvested all the trees near one spur of the railroad, they would pick up the rails and lay a new spur somewhere else. The rail lines were relatively easy to build on the sandy soil. Unlike narrow-gauge railroads often used in mining, the company used standard width tracks so they could fit as many logs as possible on each car. Russ Baehr reports the company sent 125 carloads a day to the mill in two trips.

The Shevlin-Hixon mill was on the west side of the river but its timberlands were on the east side. The company's railroad bridge crossed the river near Lava Butte, just above Benham Falls, and the company logged the area east of the river from Lava Butte on south. Grace says there was a camp about three miles east of the ranch that remained there until 1932. This was probably the Cliff Camp that appears in about that location in a report on Shevlin-Hixon camps written by Ronald Gregory.

From 1916 to the early 1930s, Shevlin-Hixon had multiple camps for its workers spread out through the logging areas and it moved the camps every few years. The workers' houses were small and narrow so they could fit on a railcar. The houses had two rooms and a wood stove in the middle. When it came time to move the camp, cranes and log loaders lifted the houses on and off the railcars. The residents were told to secure everything in the house the morning of the move. But the crane operators were so experienced there was almost no danger of damage. One family inadvertently left a coffee cup on a table before one move and found it was still there, un-spilled, when they entered the house again in the new location.

In the 1930s, the company began to use more trucks and fewer railroads. This saved the costs of building the railroads and moving the camps. In 1932, most of the Shevlin-Hixon camps were consolidated into a more permanent camp six miles east of La Pine. The houses had running water and a sewer line.

Many of the families in the Shevlin-Hixon camps had tried homesteading east of Bend in the 1910s and were forced to give up by the short growing seasons and lack of water. The men who laid the tracks, on the other hand, tended to be first- or second-generation eastern European immigrants. Some of them had stayed around after helping to build the railroad to Bend, completed in 1911. At the start of operations, there was a nucleus of people, mostly of Scandinavian ancestry, who had worked for Shevlin-Hixon's parent company in Minnesota.

The work-related buildings in the camp included the camp office, cook house and dining rooms, bath house, a saw filing shed, and a "round house" for the locomotives (which was actually a 200-foot-long rectangle). These buildings had electricity from a generator but the family houses had no electricity until four years after the camps were consolidated east of La Pine.

In the 1920s, elementary school children from the Lava Cave Camp, near the Harper Bridge over the Deschutes, attended the local Harper School. But children in the more remote camps attended elementary schools in the camps. Maude Vandevert taught in a camp east of the ranch. The schools were held in railcars 40 feet long and 16 feet wide, divided into three rooms. Shevlin-Hixon provided the railcars and the local school district provided the teachers, desks, and classroom supplies. High school students went to either Bend or La Pine. When the La Pine camp started in 1932, all the elementary and high school students were transported from the camp to La Pine schools in what was thought to be the largest school bus in Oregon. The REO Speed Wagon could hold 75 passengers.

> "When the Harper School moved to the ranch in 1929," says Grace, "there were still kids coming there from the camp. I have the pictures and knew them. I went to school in La Pine from third through sixth grade, approximately 1937 to 1941. I had girlfriends in the camp and I stayed with them probably four or five times a year. I would be invited to a Halloween party or birthday party and would ride home on their bus and stay over. These girls also came to the ranch to stay overnight. We were all very close and still have school reunions every five years. When the La Pine camp closed, after I was going to Bend to school, some of those families moved to Bend and some to the Gilchrist and Crescent area where Shevlin-Hixon was then harvesting timber. So, some of us lost track of each other. Claude and I always attended the Shevlin Camp reunion held in Bend but we have just about lost all those old friends. There were only about 20 people at the last reunion I went to.
>
> "My Mother and Dad also visited the La Pine camp. A couple of families were very special friends from the days they lived in the

camps near the ranch. The people would come to the ranch every year for a picnic and also to play music."

Shevlin employees and other people came to the ranch from as far away as La Pine and Bend to go swimming in the Little Deschutes in the summer. At the north end of the ranch, below the schoolhouse, the river made a turn to the left where the inside of the turn was shallow and warm. There was a three-acre grassy meadow with willows in it that provided families with private areas to picnic. It was easy to reach from the dirt road that ran down past the front of the schoolhouse and over a small bridge.

Across the river from the shallow area the current was faster and it cut a deep channel. The Vandeverts built two diving boards there, one close to water level and another about eight feet high. The swimming area was especially popular in the 1920s and 1930s when the Shevlin lumber camp was only about three miles away on the east side of the Dalles-California Highway.

A diving board at the Homestead.
From left to right Mary Jean, Barbara, Sallie Bird, and Grace Vandevert

In the 1920s, Claude and Pearl thought they would put in a dance floor near the swimming area and reap a little profit. They were good dancers and they both liked music.

The band consisted of four musicians. They did not practice together very much but they were good amateurs. The pick-up band also played at the Grange in La Pine and elsewhere in the area. They played popular tunes for ballroom dancing. Claude Vandevert Junior says he does not remember any square dancing.

The dance floor was about 50 yards northeast of the shallow part of the river. It was about 35 feet on a side. The Vandeverts ran a concession stand that sold hot dogs, candy, and gum. They stamped the hands of those who had paid for admission to the dance floor. Most people came as couples and then changed partners when the band played a new tune.

People would come to swim in the afternoon and stay to dance. Sometimes they would go back and forth between swimming and dancing. As the evening grew cooler, people warmed themselves at bonfires set around the dance floor. They stayed until around 11 or 12 at night.

The ranch saw three to four dances each summer and people had some memorable times. But some of the attendees drank so much they spoiled the fun for themselves and others. The dances were only held for two years. Claude and Pearl may have brought in just enough to pay the musicians and the cost of building the dance floor.

In November 1926, the family flooded the area and made a skating rink for the Bend hockey team and for the public in general. They charged admission to defray the cost of construction and lit bonfires at night for light. The ranch was suddenly more accessible to Bend residents because the Dalles-California Highway had just opened that year.

Shevlin-Hixon later moved its main timber camp south from La Pine to Crescent and ultimately to Chemult. Lois Gumpert, a friend of the Vandeverts, was the postmaster of the Shevlin post office for 10 years. She wrote, "…it seems you had to notify Washington that you were going to move to a certain place, on a certain day, at a certain hour.... I had quite a correspondence with the office of the Postmaster General because no one there could understand why a post office was going to move from Deschutes County into Klamath County. They had never heard of such a thing."

The mills harvested timber so rapidly that in 1937 the Bend Chamber of Commerce warned that the industry would collapse unless the companies started sustainable forestry. The mills were already required to replant Deschutes National Forest land after harvesting it. But they rejected sustainable forestry on land they owned. Grace says that when she rounded Lava Butte coming home from high school in the 1940s she could see for miles to the south because there were no trees to block the view. The forest has grown back since then, most of it incorporated into the Deschutes National Forest during the 1930s and 1940s and managed by the Forest Service.

By 1950, the forests were almost out of trees. Brooks-Scanlon bought the Shevlin-Hixon mill and closed it down. They cut back their own capacity over the years and finally closed their last mill in 1994.

Claude Vandevert Junior worked for a smaller lumber company, called Lelco, up until 1961. That story will be told in a later chapter.

CHAPTER 9

Sheep, Horses, and Other Animals

"We ate a lot of mutton," says Claude Vandevert Junior. "Dad wouldn't kill cattle very often. Cattle were his crop."

The Vandeverts kept a flock of sheep on the ranch from the 1920s to the 1940s. There were 30 to 40 ewes and a few rams. Income from the wool helped tide the family over during the Depression of the 1930s. The family sheared the sheep in the spring, garnering one to two sacks of wool. A wool sack, designed to ride in a truck, was about eight feet long and three feet in diameter. When a sack was full, it weighed about 500 pounds. In his younger days, Bill Vandevert could shear 100 sheep a day.

The other income from sheep was selling the lambs in fall for slaughter. The new lambs came in February and by fall they weighed 80 to 90 pounds each. A ewe that had not lambed was sold as well, though no one would pay much for a ewe. Unlike the cattle, the sheep stayed on the ranch year-round.

The economic advantage of sheep was that they would eat almost anything. Like deer, they browsed the ends of branches on bushes. In the winter, they were fed rye that was stored in the barn. They stayed outside year-round but received double their usual feed if the weather was particularly cold. If it snowed all night, the sheep would walk around in the morning with a foot of snow piled on their backs.

The sheep had to be bunched together and watched over during the day to keep the coyotes from attacking them. At night, they stayed in a three-acre pen across the river from the Homestead. The pen had gates at either end for herding the sheep in and out. The smaller milking corral was just west of it and calves that belonged to the milk cow stayed in the sheep pen. In the daytime, the sheep went to pasture in the woods or most often to an area of the ranch that the family called Cox's Bend. It was the low land west of the river and south of the Homestead. Claude Junior says there was a family named Cox in the area and speculates that they had once camped in that place. The sheep did not pasture on the rye fields after the rye was harvested because the cattle would not eat pasture that sheep had gone through. The sheep would eat the pasture unevenly and leave their smell on the ground.

The job of shepherd fell to Claude Junior. Claude carried a fishing pole much more often than he carried a rifle. The coyotes would stay hidden when Claude was around and he rarely saw them. But once, when he forgot his lunch and went back to the house for 35 minutes, the coyotes killed four sheep.

The sheep were not branded because the wool would cover up the brand. They were painted with a "turkey track" design—three prongs in the front and one prong behind. The paint was easy to see through the spring and sometimes lasted into the fall. The paint washed out after the wool was sheared. It was important to paint the sheep in case they got mixed up with one of the large flocks that went by the ranch every year.

Leona Stocking, whose grandfather, Peter Thompson, lived near the ranch in the 1910s, wrote about sheep passing through the area before Claude Junior and Grace were born. "Large flocks went by on their way to the Paulina Mountains for summer pasture. Some of these flocks were huge with 2,000 or 3,000 head in them. The sheepherders used a few dogs to help move the sheep. The Thompson children said they could hear them coming a long way off. Sometimes a straggler lamb got left behind. The children took it to Mrs. Thompson, who was able to feed it with a little warm milk and nurse it along. They grew into a small flock of perhaps nine or 10 sheep."

Grace remembers the sheep in the 1930s: "They came south past Lava Butte and along the road right outside our fence—not out on Highway 97—and they kept mostly to the road. At that time, South Century was a dirt road and we could see the dust rise when a band was coming. We watched the whole thing."

The big flocks came from as far away as Grass Valley, Grant County, and Maupin. They were on their way to summer range in the high lakes area of the Cascades. Some turned west toward the mountains on South Century a mile and a half south of the ranch. Others went further south to Crescent and Davis Lake. When Claude Junior was six or seven (in 1929 or 1930), about 20 to 25 flocks went by the ranch entrance on South Century. These flocks were as big as 1,800 sheep. The smallest had 900 sheep. Every once in a while a shepherd would leave a ewe at the ranch that was struggling to keep up with the flock. As Grace recalls:

> "The sheepherders were generally from the east Bend area or Prineville. They didn't want to take the rams (or 'bucks' as we called them) with them. The bucks tended to injure each other by butting heads and it was hard to care for them in a big herd spread out over a mountainside. We took about 20 or 30 bucks each year and kept them in a small corral just south of Kathryn Grace's grave. I suppose the sheepherders paid Dad (Claude Senior) for looking after them.
>
> "When the rams injured one another, the wounds would sometimes be infected with maggots. Dad would heat a kind of tar and paint it on the wound with a paintbrush to help it heal. It seemed to work. I've almost put it out of my mind. I hated seeing those maggots.
>
> "Then, in the fall of the year, the sheepherders came back to the north and picked up their bucks and they would sometimes camp on the ranch overnight on their way either home or headed south. Dad and I would walk up to the camp (near the small sheep corral) and I could have a biscuit with them! They were mostly Irishmen and were very respectful men. I had favorites. They had thousands of sheep in most cases.
>
> "Our own sheep were kept across the river at that time. We had our own bucks and we certainly didn't mix them with all those other

bucks. Sometimes the sheepherders would leave a 'bummer' lamb with us when headed south. A bummer was a lamb that the mother wouldn't take care of. We would feed it with a pop bottle and nipple and keep it behind the stove in the kitchen until it could join our sheep. That happened with our sheep too. We just fed it until it could get along. Sometimes, another ewe would take a bummer.

"We ate lamb regularly, and my Mother canned a lot of it. She made lamb stew, lamb chops (when first killed), roasts and other dishes like hash. Lamb chops were delicious. But I never eat lamb anymore—probably haven't had any for years. I don't know what that means, but I guess I just loved the 'home-cooking'—and have never found it again." (Or perhaps Grace ate a lifetime's worth of lamb while she still lived on the ranch.)

Grace only half remembers the family raising a pig every year. "I think the pen was across the big bridge on the other side of the river." But Grace remembers very well how good the pork chops and roasts were. "I think we butchered in the fall. Dad did it all down by the old garage with a big barrel of hot water to clean the hair off. He always 'smoked' the hindquarters to make bacon. The 'smoke' was simply a liquid that he painted on. Then he hung the meat in the guestroom above the kitchen where it became bacon. We made lots of sausage and used it for breakfast meat all the time."

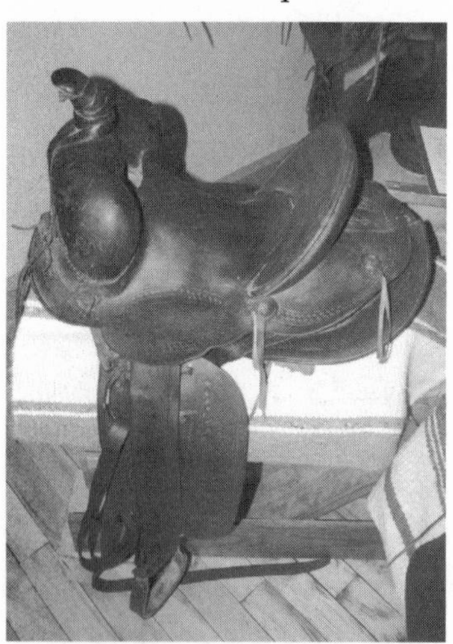

Claude Senior rode Major and other horses with this saddle—now at the Des Chutes Historical Museum.

At any one time, there were about six or eight horses on the ranch. There were work horses, a riding horse for each member of the family, and one or two extras. Until Claude Senior bought a tractor in early 1950, he always had at least two teams of work horses. The work horses mowed hay, pulled wagons, and did other heavy work. The teams that Grace remembers from her childhood were Pearl and Ruby and then Molly and Skipper. They were steady old horses that Grace could handle even as a young girl.

The riding horses were necessary for driving the cattle to and from the summer range and for keeping an eye on the cattle year-round. Early on, Bill Vandevert rode horses while bear hunting or marking new trails in the Cascades.

Grace's mother had a white horse before Grace was born. Pearl loved to ride. Claude Senior had a horse named Major. Major was purchased by Clint Vandevert in eastern Oregon. Clint had been hunting on the horse and liked the way he could shoot from the saddle. He bought the horse from the man who told him that Major had been an Army horse.

Claude Junior remembers a very special horse he once had:

> "When I was about eight or nine years old, in 1931 or 1932, Dad's brother Bill decided I needed my own horse. So he gave me a colt named Pepper that his mare, Queen, had foaled that spring. Uncle Bill kept him for a couple years, broke him to ride, and then turned him over to me. Because Pepper was a quarter hot blood (a term we used for thoroughbreds), Dad wouldn't let me ride him for a couple years. Finally I felt that I could handle him and from that time on he was the only horse I rode. We spent a lot of time in the saddle because we had cattle to watch over and care for.
>
> "I can't give you detailed information about the lineage of Queen, Uncle Bill's horse, but I'm sure Uncle Bill was correct in saying that she was a descendant of Man O' War." Man O'War was born in 1917 and was voted the greatest United States trained thoroughbred racehorse of all time. Just after World War I, he won 20 of his 21 races. His descendants included Seabiscuit and War Admiral. One of Man O'War's grandfathers happened to be called Bend Or. But Bend Or was a British horse that didn't have anything to do with Bend or with Oregon.
>
> "Queen's other lineage could have been Arabian or quarter-horse. Uncle Bill raised thoroughbreds for several years and lineage was extremely important to him. So I suspect he could actually have traced Queen's ancestry.

"Pepper was what we called a strawberry roan. The red or bay color was faded to almost a pink and mixed with white. He had completely white legs to above the knees. He was not a big horse compared with the usual saddle horses used for riding after cattle. Even though he was small—perhaps 60 to 64 inches—he could pack a rider for 14 to 16 hours and accomplish a lot of work during that time. He was high-spirited and you had to be a good rider to stay with him. He never bucked, but when he saw a cow try to break away from the herd, he took off before the rider even saw what was going on.

"Pepper had been well broken to ride, but his spirit had never been broken. There was not a mean streak anywhere in him. One time we were trying to head off a cow that had broken away from the herd and he was on a dead run when all of a sudden he planted all four feet and slid to a stop. I was hanging on to anything I could grasp to stay with him. When we came to a stop, there was a wire stretched between two trees about a foot in front of my neck. He had seen it but I had not. From that time on we had a real love affair!"

Claude continues,

"I never raced Pepper against another horse, but he was faster than other horses I had ridden. I have no idea how many generations he was removed from Man O' War, but I suspect several. He was born in the early 1930s, so that would make possibly 13 or 14 years after his great sire.

"During the winter, we turned the horses out of the ranch and let them fend for themselves in open range south of the ranch. Sounds like we didn't take care of them as we should have, but they always came out of the winter in better shape than if we had them closed up. The slough bottoms in the winter provided a lot of good feed for horses and it did save some of the harvested hay for the cattle. Hay was always in short supply for the winter feeding

"The horses seemed to like to find their own food. Even when they were on the ranch, they sometimes didn't come to the barn area for feed. When the winter got too bad for them they would come home for a while and we would feed them.

"I rode Pepper until in my late teens. One summer, a horse raiser offered me $500 for him, but I told him Pepper was not for sale. The following winter was the last time we ever saw Pepper. We searched all over Central Oregon and had others looking for us all over the Northwest, but to no avail. The guy who had offered to buy Pepper had a pretty shady reputation. I always suspected him but of course couldn't prove anything."

Grace talks about two horses she had that died from misfortunes on the ranch and nearby. "The first horse was a Shetland pony—black and white—that we called Dolly. That was when I was about seven or eight years old. I rode her both with and without a saddle and drove my Aunt Dorothy crazy—she thought I would get killed! Nope—I was fine:

"We had to keep the ice open for the cattle and horses in the winter time so they could drink water. We had a little shallow area connected to the river in back of where the "new" house is now. Dolly evidently came to drink one evening and there was ice on the top of the water. I don't know what happened, but she somehow got into the water and ice and couldn't get out. Dad found her there the next morning. I think she had died by then, but I never asked. Dad had to get the team of horses to help drag her out and I don't know how he disposed of her. Claude and I probably were off to school across the field.

"Then Dad bought a strawberry roan mare that I called Nellie—and she was my horse from then on. I could ride her anywhere. I had a friend that lived near Bates Butte and she would ride down to visit me on her horse. Then we would go riding together. We were left up to our own devices and it was great fun. I'd take Nellie as far as where the Sunriver Lodge is now—would go as far as the Harper Bridge (over the Big Deschutes on Spring River Road) and out to get the mail on Highway 97. When the war came along and all the soldiers were around, Dad restricted me to riding just inside our property. So, I would just go down by the schoolhouse and back and around the ranch area.

"Then we lost three horses out on the railroad track—just north of the Vandevert Road crossing. I remember because one of them was Nellie. I don't remember how the horses got themselves out of the ranch. The horses had gone into a cut where the tracks ran below

> ground level just north of Vandevert Road. The train engineer told Dad the horses had tried to climb out but the cut was too steep. The engineer could not slow down the train quickly enough to stop or to give the horses more time to escape. The railroad company paid Dad for the loss because they were supposed to have the tracks fenced off by then. This was probably about 1945."

Bill Vandevert kept bear hounds for hunting but, over the history of the ranch, the primary dogs were shepherds bred for herding cattle. The family generally had one dog at a time and the working dogs also became pets. The first one Grace can remember was Tippy, a little brown and black female. The second was Nick, a black and white male. There was an Australian Shepherd after that whose name is lost to history.

The dogs were particularly important driving the cattle to and from their summer range. Claude Vandevert Senior moved the cattle to the summer range in May. Some of the cattle did not want to leave the ranch, especially the younger ones who did not know where they were going. As the herd moved along, individual cows started to wander off on their own. The men on horseback would sic the dog after them. Tippy or Nick got in front of the cow, barking and snapping, until the cow turned its head and ambled back to the herd. It meant the men on horseback could direct the herd without having to chase after the errant cows.

Mary Jean wrote, "Sometimes we would hear this sad noise and go in the dining room to find one of the dogs standing on his hind legs at the window and waiting for us because they had been entangled with a porcupine. It seems to me it was very brave and smart of them to come to us because they knew it was going to hurt to have those quills removed. But they knew they would at least get rid of them. We would slide back the window, bring the pliers, and start pulling out each quill, one by one. The quills were mostly in their noses but sometimes in their feet and legs."

The dogs were not allowed in the house, though they sometimes stuck their heads in the door. They lived off table scraps and what they could find on their own—often deer and other animals that had died.

The dogs liked chasing sage rats, but they were not very successful at catching them. When the dogs could not find things to eat, the family made up some coarse bread with bacon fat or cracklings from rendering fat out of beef. The dogs were never on a leash and enjoyed the freedom to go and do what they pleased. The family all agreed the dogs had a good life.

The chicken coop, between the Homestead and the barn, was long and narrow with entrances at both ends. One half of the building was for chickens and the other half was for the turkeys. Whoever went to feed them and gather eggs walked in the door to a small feed room with all the grain, then through another door to the chicken roost, and then another door to the turkeys. There were maybe 10 or 15 chickens and about six or eight turkeys. The family ate most of the eggs but sold some of them for cash. The birds did not have a lot of personality except for the turkey gobbler, the big male turkey. He was aggressive and would chase Grace when she got near the coop.

There was a lot of life on the ranch, wild and domesticated. But the most interesting lived in the house.

CHAPTER 10

Ranch Life in the 1930s

Every fall a large group of Indians visited the ranch with their children. As Grace tells it:

"They would come in the morning by car and have horses and supplies with them. There were probably about thirty adults because I think they pitched about four or five tents in the upper pasture. They were there for about two weeks hunting deer. It was a fascinating time for me. Whole families came with their children and even with little babies, called papooses. The men would go hunting and bring back the deer meat and hides. The women would prepare the hides for tanning and making moccasins, gloves, clothing and many other things.

"When the men came in from their hunt they built a sweat house made of willows bent over to form a dome-shaped little room. They would heat rocks in a fire outside the house until they were very hot. Then they would dump the rocks into buckets of water they brought from the river. This would heat up the lodge like a sauna and they would sit there for some time. When they were done they would run out of the little house stark, staring naked and go jump in the river! They were very healthy people so I guess this did them a lot of good besides giving them a good bath. I wasn't allowed up at the camp when all this was going on. I got to go 'skinny dipping' all the time but not when anyone else was around.

"We provided the Indians with fresh milk every day. The Indian children would come down in the evening, come in the house and just sort of sit and listen. It was hard to get them to talk. But they would

> bring a papoose with them and I got to hold it in its cradle. It was a wonderful experience!
>
> "My grampa was very good to the Indians and they loved him. The older men of the tribe would come to visit him in the living room and talk about old days. Grampa could speak a lot of their language. I heard a little of it but mostly stayed out of the way. The Indians would leave just as they arrived—very quickly and quietly. The Indians were very respectful of other people's property. When they left it was hard to tell they had ever been there."

No one knows for sure where the Indians came from or which tribe they belonged to. The closest Indians were on the Warm Springs Indian Reservation about 75 miles to the north. Russ Baehr says they were always on the move. But another possibility is that they came from somewhere near Cottage Grove, Oregon. Bill's mother, Grace Clark Vandevert, dedicated herself to the welfare of the Indians near her home there where Bill grew up. Indians visiting from there might have known Bill Vandevert from their childhood and he might have learned some of their language.

In 1931, Pearl wrote to her aunt, "Claude (Senior) is busy building a wagon bridge across the river. We have a footbridge but haven't had a bigger bridge for years as we use the county bridge about a half mile from here." The county bridge was at the north end of the ranch where

The wagon bridge was partially rebuilt later to be a dock for the Homestead.

the road that passed the schoolhouse went over the Little Deschutes. A few years after Claude Senior built the new wagon bridge near the Homestead, the river rose above both it and the footbridge. Claude Senior tied a rowboat to the back porch so he could get across the river and milk the cows. The milk cows were sometimes milked in the milking corral across the river and sometimes in the shed beside the barn.

There was an old land-locked channel west of the river opposite the Homestead. In the winter, it filled with water and froze, making it perfect for skating. Grace remembers, "Claude would always put my 'clamp-on' skates on my boots and away we would go! We could skate on the river too, but you had to be more cautious due to the current of the river."

The icehouse was also across the river, downstream a bit, on the west bank. "The icehouse walls were filled with sawdust for insulation," says Grace. "My father and brother cut blocks of ice out of the river when it froze and dragged them up a wooden slide by hand. We covered each layer of ice with a layer of sawdust and then all the ice was covered with six inches more. The ice would last until September. A delicious part of any summer get-together at the ranch was homemade ice cream. It was hand-cranked and required a lot of chopped ice and salt to keep it really cold while turning. The flavor was always vanilla."

A big occasion for ice cream was the Fourth of July picnic held in the pine trees north of the ice house. Arthur Vandevert and his family were always there from Kentucky. All the family members in the area, and many friends of the family, came to the picnic. Claude Senior barbecued and everyone brought food. The family hung a large American Flag. The Fourth of July was also Grace's birthday and it took many years for her to realize the surrounding holiday was Independence Day.

The lodgepole pines on the west side of the river supplied the wood for the stoves and the fireplace at the Homestead. In the 1930s, Claude Senior and Junior cut and trimmed the wood in the forest and hauled it to the house in an old flatbed ranch truck. They ran a belt from the back wheel of an old Model T Ford to a buzz saw that cut the wood to the desired lengths. The wood was then stacked in the woodshed at the back of the house. Every day, they chopped up several blocks of wood for the cook stove in the kitchen. In the winter, they chopped up more wood for the stoves and fireplace that heated the house. They filled the kitchen wood box to overflowing so Pearl would not have to go out and get more wood before they came home. Everybody pitched in to help carry in the wood.

Well into Grace's childhood, the family repaired their own shoes, putting on new soles when they old ones wore out. There was a room above the stairs called the "Shoe Shop." It was entered by pulling a plank out of the room, bracing it against a step, and walking up the plank.

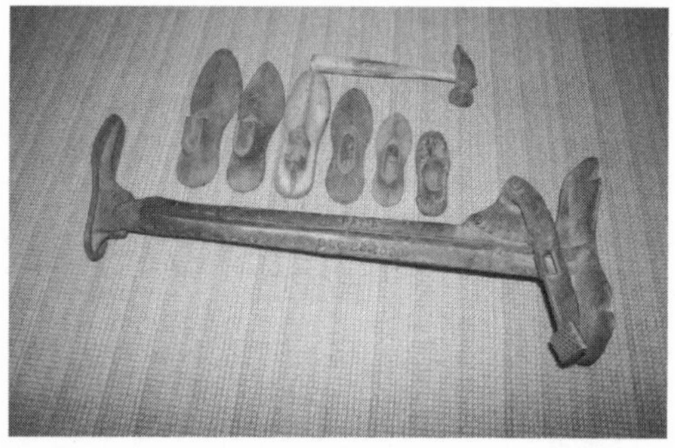

The family's shoe stand with multiple shoe forms for repairing and re-soling shoes.

The family always had meat but vegetables and fruit were sometimes limited. Grace says,

> "All the years I was there, we had a vegetable garden. The latter years, it was just across the big bridge from the house and it was about 125 feet by 30 feet in size. It was fenced in so the calves couldn't get into it.
>
> "We had almost all the 'root' veggies—turnips, rutabaga, onions, parsnips, beets, and a few others. Those did very well except when the summer was cool they were on the small size. Dad (Claude Senior) also put in potatoes. They grew to about the size of lemons and were so good. We cooked them with the peelings on. We also had spinach, kohlrabi (sort of like cabbage in taste), and Swiss chard. What we didn't have were things like peas, corn, and green beans. They couldn't

survive the hard freeze that happened about once a month in the spring and summer. I don't know where the family got those vegetables before the railroad came to Bend. We had to buy them at the store in cans. I do know that Redmond had a warmer growing season and I think we obtained some of those vegetables from farmers down there. When Uncle Bill lived in Tumalo I believe he could grow some peas. He was also able to grow strawberries and sold them—so it was definitely warmer. We would buy crates of things like apricots, pears, apples and can them all."

In 1936, Pearl wrote to her Aunt Linnie, "Haven't even started to get caught up with my work yet and am still swamped. Counted my jars and had over 380 jars of everything. I only had about 100 when you were here so you can see I have been on the jump. One week put up over 120 jars of jelly and jam besides canning lots of other things. Have about a box and a half of pears to can then think I will quit." Grace says,

Grace with her catch of the day. Footbridge and pasture fence in background.

"I would think my grandmother Sadie would have grown everything she could get her hands on. They got their fruit each year from the Willamette Valley area. They picked huckleberries up around Taylor Burn and further south and would go for over-night trips to gather them. They also got wild plums from Summer Lake. I remember the plums but can barely remember going after them.

"The best mushrooms we ever ate were back from the river on the west side in a meadow among the jack pine. They were huge and tasty. There was just one kind, the white button ones you buy at the store, but at the ranch they grew big. We thought it was a great treat to have mushrooms. Dad always fried them in bacon grease and I can still remember how good they were. We had one that was so big it fit in a galvanized washtub and we took it to Bend to Mr. Cashman at his men's clothing store. He and Mr. Magill, the druggist, used to drive out to the ranch just to pick mushrooms. Dad let them—they were all close friends.

"My mother baked bread almost every day. But sometimes, like on wash-day, she could not handle it all. She put the dough out to rise on top of the stove by the stove pipe where it was warm and toasty. The bread took about an hour to rise depending on the temperature. Then, she had to 'punch' it down and make the loaves that she put in two pans and let rise again. She made, I believe, six loaves at a time. Then she put them in the oven.

The family's Home Comfort wood stove—now at the Des Chutes Historical Museum.

"The bread would usually be baked and ready to eat by early afternoon. It probably was the best smell in the world to come home to. It drove us crazy while it was baking. We got to eat some while it was still hot. Then, Mom would give a loaf to anyone who was visiting to take home. She sometimes made a pan of rolls for the dinner meal and other times, cinnamon rolls. She did not make wheat bread very often. It depended on how much time she had.

"We ate our meals in the kitchen. My Dad built the kitchen table and always said that it was just the size to 'reach across easily.' (The table and the Home Comfort wood stove are now in the Des Chutes Historical Museum in Bend.)

"The dining room table was about four feet square when it had no leaves in it. We only used it for eating when we had big family dinners. But we used it all the time for everything else. I would sit in one corner in the evening, Claude in the other, my Dad at the other end and my Mother as close to the gas lamp in the center as she could get! She would be doing mending like darning sox. Claude and I had to do our homework so it was pretty quiet. Our only radio was in that room and, if everything else was done, we could listen to the programs.

"We had a single gas lamp that had a porcelain shade. It used white gas, like a Coleman camping lantern, and gave off a good bright light, the best in the house. We also used the white gas to run the washing machine in the laundry room. It was cleaner than kerosene. We used the gas lamp in the kitchen for our meals at night. Then we cleaned the kitchen and moved the lamp onto the dining room table.

"We also had about three kerosene lamps going at once in the evening. We needed a kerosene lamp left in the kitchen because we still went back and forth during the evening. My Mother could put an old type curling iron down the chimney of a kerosene lamp and heat it up to curl her hair. We had to wash the chimneys of the kerosene lamps about once a week because they got smoky.

"We usually lit the kerosene lamps downstairs and took them up when we went to bed. I tried to read books by them until my folks would make me go to sleep. If we put our pajamas on downstairs, we could run upstairs without a lamp and just go to bed. In the winter it was too cold for anything else! We used kerosene lanterns to go do the milking in the winter time. The lamps were not risky as long as you used common sense. I do not remember any accidents.

"We never used candles. I'm sure Dad would have thought they would be dangerous. We had some around but not for regular use. We always had a flashlight or two. There were lots of 'dark' corners of that old house and we would use a flashlight if necessary at night. People visiting us would use them to go to the outhouse but we knew the way without them."

Music was always around from a battery radio, a phonograph, or someone playing the piano. Claude and Pearl liked popular music from the 1910s and 1920s. Grace still has her mother's sheet music, including the following titles:

- All the World Will be Jealous of Me
- An Old Fashioned Wife
- Everybody Loves to Dance
- Hindustan
- I May be Gone for a Long, Long Time
- I Want One Like Pa Had Yesterday
- I'm in Love with a Mystic Shriner

- Just a Baby's Prayer at Twilight (For her Daddy Over There)
- Little Mother of Mine
- Mandalay (from Musical Settings of Rudyard Kipling's Barrack Room Ballads)
- My Mother's Rosary
- On the Road to Home Sweet Home
- She's the Daughter of Mother Machree
- So Long Letty
- Sweet Little Buttercup
- There are Fairies at the Bottom of Our Garden
- You'll Always be the Same Sweet Baby

Claude Senior could play the harmonica, but he loved light opera and violin music in particular. The couple brought lots of sheet music and 12-inch 78-RPM records with them when they moved to the ranch from Portland in 1922. The records included Hawaiian music and Sousa marches. The family played Sousa a lot and marched around the living room. The piano came as a gift from Uncle Bill in 1926.

The family first had a tall phonograph with the turntable in the top. In the 1930s, one of Claude's brothers gave the family a phonograph that was built like a table and also had room in the bottom for records. It is still in the family.

Sometimes on Sunday evenings, Pearl played the piano and the family gathered around to sing songs. Claude Junior says it was a great

The piano from the Homestead is now in the common room in the barn above the stables.

way to grow up. The kids had good relationships with each other and with their parents.

A friend and neighbor who lived about a mile away, Lois Maker Gumpert, came to the house in the 1930s for an evening of music. Her father played a banjo and other instruments while Lois played the piano. Johnny Brasel played the saw. He placed a regular cutting saw across his knee and used a bow to play it. Lois could play up a storm. Well into her 80s she played piano for the Kiwanis Club in Bend every week.

In recent years, the family piano was acquired by the current homeowners through the Vandevert Ranch Association and has a place of honor in the meeting room on the second floor of the new barn.

The whole family went to dances at the little Pioneer Hall in La Pine about once a month in the winter. A small live band played waltzes, one steps, two steps, and lots of square dancing. Claude Senior's friends would help the kids learn to square dance. The dances went as late as 1:30 in the morning. They would light a fire in the dining room stove when they got home so everyone could get warm enough to go to bed and not freeze.

The family traveled to dances at Pioneer Hall in La Pine.

"When I was in high school, I got my father to take me to those dances in La Pine again," says Grace. "I had one boyfriend who lived in Chemult. We would spend the night dancing together then he would go home in his car back to Chemult and I would go home with Dad. Later, we had two nighttime dates. He came to the ranch and I think he liked to talk to my Dad as much as he liked seeing me!"

Claude Junior, Grace, and Mary Jean loved all the Hit Parade tunes of the day. They would buy a hit song magazine every month just to learn all the words.

Pearl's relatives gave her books and she borrowed more from the Bend library. But Grace does not see how her mother had much time to read them. Grace thinks most of the books were novels, but Pearl had a whole set of James Whitcomb Riley poetry. Claude Senior did not read many books, but he read two newspapers every day and was a loyal fan of the crossword puzzles. He read the comics to Grace every night when she was young.

Music and reading were big parts of the children's lives. Every month, the school would change the books in the school library and Grace tried to read every new one that came in. Sometimes she would sneak a book out of the house and read it sitting in the hay in the barn. No one could interrupt her to remind her to do her chores.

Magazines were much more popular before television than they are now. The family received five or six a month, including the Saturday Evening Post, National Geographic, Reader's Digest, and at least one women's magazine. Grace says there was always something in the mail. People wrote and received more letters then. Phone calls were expensive.

Irvin S. Cobb, the famous American humorist, remembered Bill Vandevert from writing about his bear hunt in Newberry Crater. Cobb came back to visit the ranch when Grace was a child and sat out on the front porch with Bill. Grace's nanny goat climbed up onto the roof of Mr. Cobb's car and stood there looking at the people on the porch. Grace was very afraid the goat would scratch the car. But Mr. Cobb thought it was very funny and said he would never forget his visit. Grace says the black-and-white goat "wouldn't mind me at all. I wanted to have her play with me—follow me—go where I went—all for naught. She was totally stubborn. I think we took her back to where we got her."

In the late 1920s, the man who had faced down grizzly bears was hit by a car at an intersection in Portland. When they took Bill Vandevert to the hospital, they said that nearly every bone in his body was broken. He was in the hospital for a long time and he could no longer help with the outside work when he finally came back to the ranch. He used a cane from then on. In his later years, he spent the winters in Bend at the home of his doctor son Clint.

But Bill returned to the ranch every summer until he was 88 years old. His son, Claude Senior, built a little cabin for him next to the house because he had trouble getting up the stairs to his old room. The cabin had a bed, a dresser, and a small wood stove. Grace reports,

Bill Vandevert with his cane. He was struck by an automobile in Portland in 1928 and could no longer do ranch work.

> "I was sort of in charge of his little cabin. Once a week, I would chase him out to the front porch and I would tear apart his bed, change it, and clean the floor and put things away. He had a little stove and we all brought wood to him for that—every day or so—and put it on his little porch. When he would come back to his cabin, he would always make a big thing out of my cleaning it for him — 'My, my, isn't that nice?' kind of thing—and it made me feel good. Dad took care of him, too, as did my Mother. He came into the kitchen for his three meals a day and sat in the same place. He sometimes started talking about something and we listened, but we were able to say things at the table even if we were kids in those days. It was a good family time. He ate well and would sometimes say something was extra good.
>
> "We would take him to Bend with us and he would enjoy visiting his old buddies in front of the Magill Drug Store and the O'Kane Building and that is where we would pick him up to take him back home. He read the *Bend Bulletin* every day."

William Plutarch Vandevert lived over 90 years. He died on February 26, 1944, and is buried in Greenwood Cemetery in Bend. The Masonic Lodge conducted the service.

CHAPTER 11

Heat, Light, and Civilization

"We never called it 'The Homestead' in my day," says Grace. "Old-timers sometimes did. But our mail came to 'The Old Homestead, Bend, Oregon' when I was small. Then it became 'Up River Route' and finally, the address became Vandevert Road. When my mother first came to the ranch, she had stationary that said 'The Old Homestead.' It seems funny today because the house was only 30 years old when she came there. But the ranch was a real landmark back then because it had been in the area longer than anything else."

The ranch mailbox was a mile away on U.S. Highway 97 for over 60 years, from the time the highway was built in 1926 until the developers of the new Vandevert Ranch persuaded the post office to move the mailbox to the front gate in the 1990s. The Vandeverts rode a horse or drove a car out to the mailbox every morning to get the mail and the *Bend Bulletin*.

The road that runs along the east side of the ranch has been called Century Drive or South Century Drive as long as anyone can remember. Nielsen, Newman, and McCart, in their book, *Pioneer Roads in Central Oregon*, say the old Huntington Road, built in 1867, ran about half a mile east of South Century. Perhaps Huntington ran where Blue Eagle Road is today. Grace says that Huntington Road was also known as the Immigrant Road in the area of the ranch because it was followed by the Elliott party of 1853, a train of 250 wagons and over 1,000 people that got lost and suffered hard times while trying to reach the Willamette Valley.

Leona Stocking, whose grandfather Peter owned the long-gone Harper Hotel near the ranch, wrote about the building of South Century in the 1910s, "The road was being built from Harper to Lava Butte. Peter's eldest son Tom (born 1895) worked with the crew. They had to dynamite a lot of big stumps, some as large as 40 inches across. They would put a whole box of dynamite under the stump, light the fuse and run for cover. The blast blew the stump in pieces high in the air and left a hole in the ground big enough to drop a team of horses into."

There was no good road south to Klamath Falls until the Dalles-California Highway was built in 1926. It ran from The Dalles on the Columbia River down to Weed in Northern California. U.S. Highway 97, which today runs south from the Canadian border, incorporates the Dalles-California Highway from about 60 miles south of The Dalles all the way to Weed. Even after the highway was built, stretches of it were unpaved dirt. Vandevert Road was built after The Dalles-California Highway was completed. The road runs between South Century and Highway 97. For all of Grace's childhood the road did not have a name. There was just a sign out on Highway 97 that pointed the way to Fall River, Pringle Falls, and South Century Drive. Grace says, "I wasn't living on the ranch when the road was named Vandevert and the county assigned address numbers. I know we all had fun with the new name. But Dad wasn't too thrilled with it being named Vandevert Road. He was a man who didn't want a fuss about his name or his status as an old-timer."

There were two or three families and a couple of woodcutters who lived on the Big Deschutes and used a road, now gone, that went by the schoolhouse and over the Little Deschutes on a county bridge. Until Claude Senior built a wagon bridge on the ranch in 1931 the family used the county bridge to take wagons to the west part of the ranch.

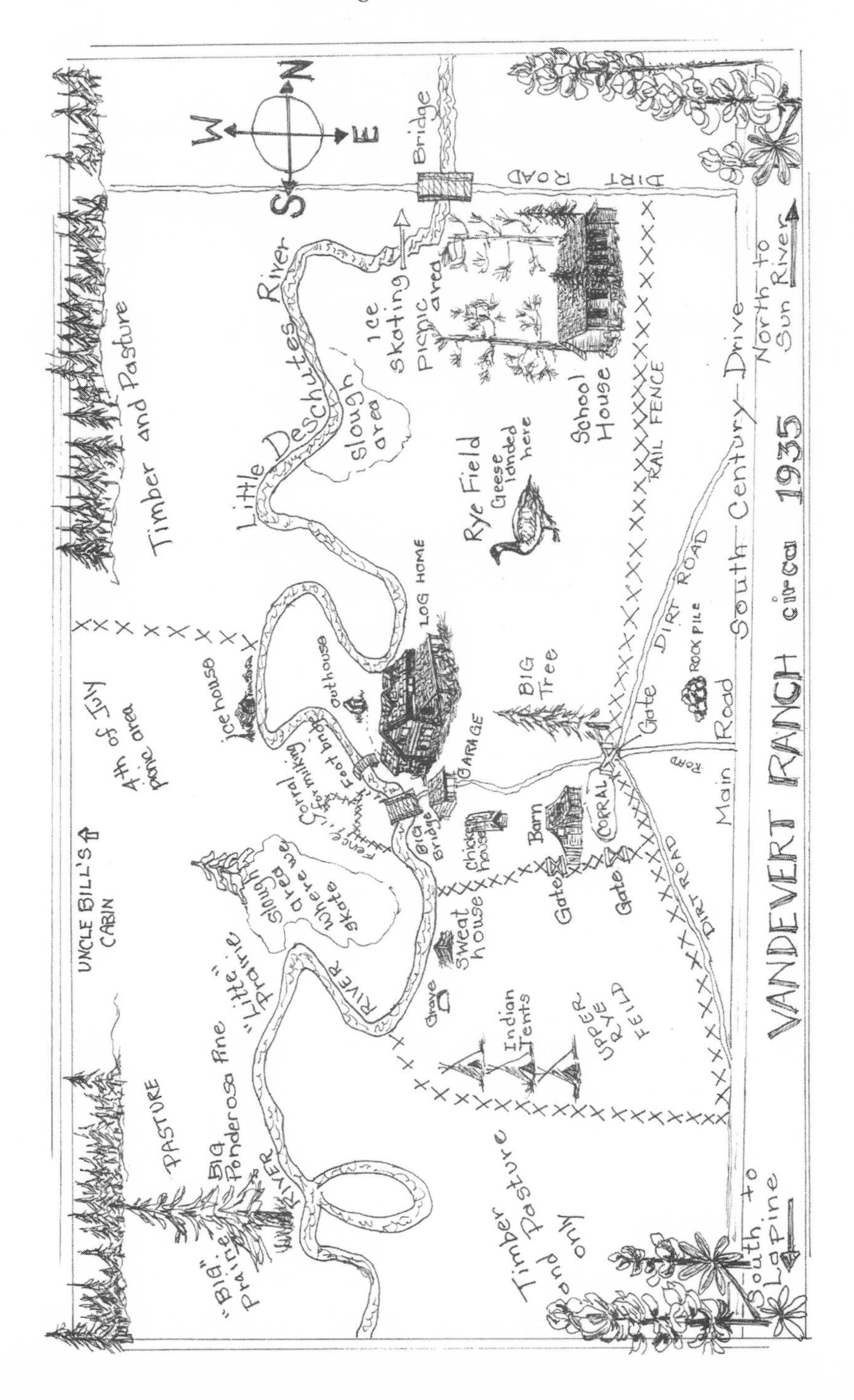
VANDEVERT RANCH circa 1935
W
E
N
S
Bridge
DIRT ROAD
Timber and Pasture
Little Deschutes River
Ice skating
picnic area
slough area
Rye Field
Geese landed here
School House
RAIL FENCE
North to Sun River
South Century Drive
DIRT ROAD
ROCK PILE
Main Road
LOG HOME
BIG Tree
4th of July picnic area
ice house
outhouse
Corral for milking
Foot bridge
Fence
GARAGE
BIG Bridge
chick house
Barn
CORRAL
Gate
Gate
Gate
Gate
ROAD
DIRT ROAD
UNCLE BILL'S CABIN
slough area where we skate
"Little" Prairie
Sweat house
RIVER
Grave
Indian Tents
UPPER RYE FEILD
PASTURE
Big Ponderosa Pine
RIVER
"Big" Prairie
Timber Pasture and only
South to LaPine

There were only 8,000 automobiles in the United States in 1900. By 1927, Henry Ford had sold 15 million Model T's for as little as $290. One of those Model T's belonged to the Vandeverts. Claude Junior says they had the car before he was born in 1923. Twenty miles per hour was considered fast in those days, especially on the dirt roads surrounding the ranch. The family used the car to visit Bend and La Pine—and to go back and forth between the Homestead and Uncle Bill's ranch at Paulina Prairie. They also jacked up the car and used a belt around a rear wheel to power a saw that cut up logs for firewood.

There was no direct rail connection from Bend south to Chemult until May of 1928. Trains from California going to Portland came north through Klamath Falls but turned west at Chemult, crossed the Little Deschutes, and climbed over the Willamette Pass. Part of the economic justification for finally building the rail link between Bend and Chemult was undoubtedly the opportunity to carry Shevlin-Hixon's logs to the mill in Bend from the forests near La Pine and, later, near Gilchrist and Chemult.

One technology the family acquired long before electricity was a telephone. It was a tall wooden phone that hung on the wall and had a crank. Modern readers might assume that ranchers and farmers far from town would be the last people to get telephone service. But telephones were highly prized by rural people because of the time, effort, and cost it took to go see someone in person. Many of them were so eager to have a telephone they formed their own telephone companies. The Dorris Telephone Company, in a rural area 140 miles south of the ranch, once served only 65 customers, including 14 farms on one single line. The company has grown into the Cal-Ore Telephone Company that serves Klamath Falls, Tulelake, Dorris, Yreka, and other small locations in the rural state border area.

"We had maybe six or eight other parties on the line," says Grace. "Uncle Bill's phone was on the same line. Our ring was one long ring and two shorts. His was one long and three shorts."

The entire time the Vandevert family lived in the Homestead, they cooked on a wood-burning kitchen stove and heated the house with four more wood stoves and a fireplace. Naturally, house fires were a constant worry. Where each stovepipe went through the first floor ceiling, the hole it went through was four inches wider than the pipe. The pipe went through the second floor ceiling and into the attic the same way. The top of the pipe was covered to keep the rain from coming in.

Claude Junior says he cannot remember his father ever lighting a fire without looking up the pipe to check that nothing was catching fire and no smoke was leaking. Only once was he sent to pour a pitcher of water on something that was smoking on the second floor. Attention to detail and perhaps the intercession of a higher power are the reasons Claude Junior gives for the absence of a house fire during the long life of the Homestead. If a fire had started in the house, the family would have dashed to the river for water.

In 1941, Pearl wrote her Aunt Linnie, "We got a bargain on a Kohler plant (electricity generator) so [we] just got it. Still can hardly believe we have it. It is a 1,500 watt and 110-volt plant, so we can run anything with it. Have only had it running since the 25th of May. Will get a different motor for my washing machine and an iron at once." Pearl had waited a long time for electricity. The people in Bend had electricity 31 years earlier.

The generator was surplus from a school in Tumalo. It was expensive to run and the batteries needed to start it were especially dear. It cost about a dollar to have electricity for an evening, so the family did not run it that often and still used white gas and kerosene lanterns for light. The electric iron was a big improvement over the heavy irons heated on the stove.

In the late 1940s, Claude Senior, using his youthful experience with the Northwest Electric Company, helped establish the Midstate Electrical Cooperative in an area that extended from Lava Butte to Christmas Valley and Klamath Marsh. Midstate was incorporated in 1948 and first delivered power in 1952 to 153 members. In 2008, Midstate delivered power to 18,000 member/owners. The co-op went from seven miles to 2,300 miles of "energized line." Having inexpensive power constantly available was a big change for the family. For the first time, they could have a refrigerator.

The fresh-water spring that had sparked the gunfight before the Vandeverts arrived was about 75 feet from the northwest corner of the barn. It stopped running about the time Claude Junior was born in 1923. The family believes the spring dried up because so many trees were harvested east of the ranch. Without the mature trees to shade it, the snow melted quickly and ran off the surface of the ground, rather than melting slowly and seeping into the water table. The developer of the modern ranch, Jim Gardner, attempted to dig the spring back to life around 1990 but could not find any water. Once the spring was gone, the family pumped its drinking water by hand from a sandpoint well sunk through the back porch. A sandpoint well is simply a pipe with a sharpened end and holes in the pipe covered with a mesh. The family had to drive the pipe only 13 feet into the sandy soil to get reliable drinking water. For water they were not going to drink, the family drew water from the Little Deschutes.

Mary Jean writes, "I took my bath in a rectangular tin tub with hot water from a huge copper boiler on the stove. Most of my baths were on Saturday night. I remember good music while taking my bath so that must have been when the New York Philharmonic or the New York Operas were on. In the summer my baths were in the river."

The Homestead did not have running water or central heat until it was rebuilt in the late 1980s.

CHAPTER 12

Politics, Religion, Liquor, and Values

Grace did not need her co-author to write this chapter. All of it comes directly from her.

My grandmother, Sadie, may have been the last Democrat in the family. My father said it helped her get the post office at the ranch. That was in 1893 when Grover Cleveland, a Democrat, was president.

From then on, the Vandevert family was Republican. At least, that is what I remember. As for my mother's family, the Catlows, I assume that they were Republican. I got that message when I visited Iowa in 2007 and met our relatives. One of my mother's letters that the family gave me was written right after Franklin Roosevelt, a Democrat, was elected president the first time in 1932.

My mother wrote, "How did you like the election? We didn't like it at all, but we hope that most of the people knew best."

Politics were at the center of a lot of the conversations between my Dad and his brothers when they were together. I do not remember the women entering into the conversations that were held, but the men had very definite opinions as to what was right and what was wrong with the world.

I thought I should be a Republican, too. So, when Wendell Willkie ran against Roosevelt in 1942, I told the kids at school I hoped Willkie would win. Well, I got laughed at by some of them—and I learned to keep my mouth closed in the future. Willkie lost to Roosevelt.

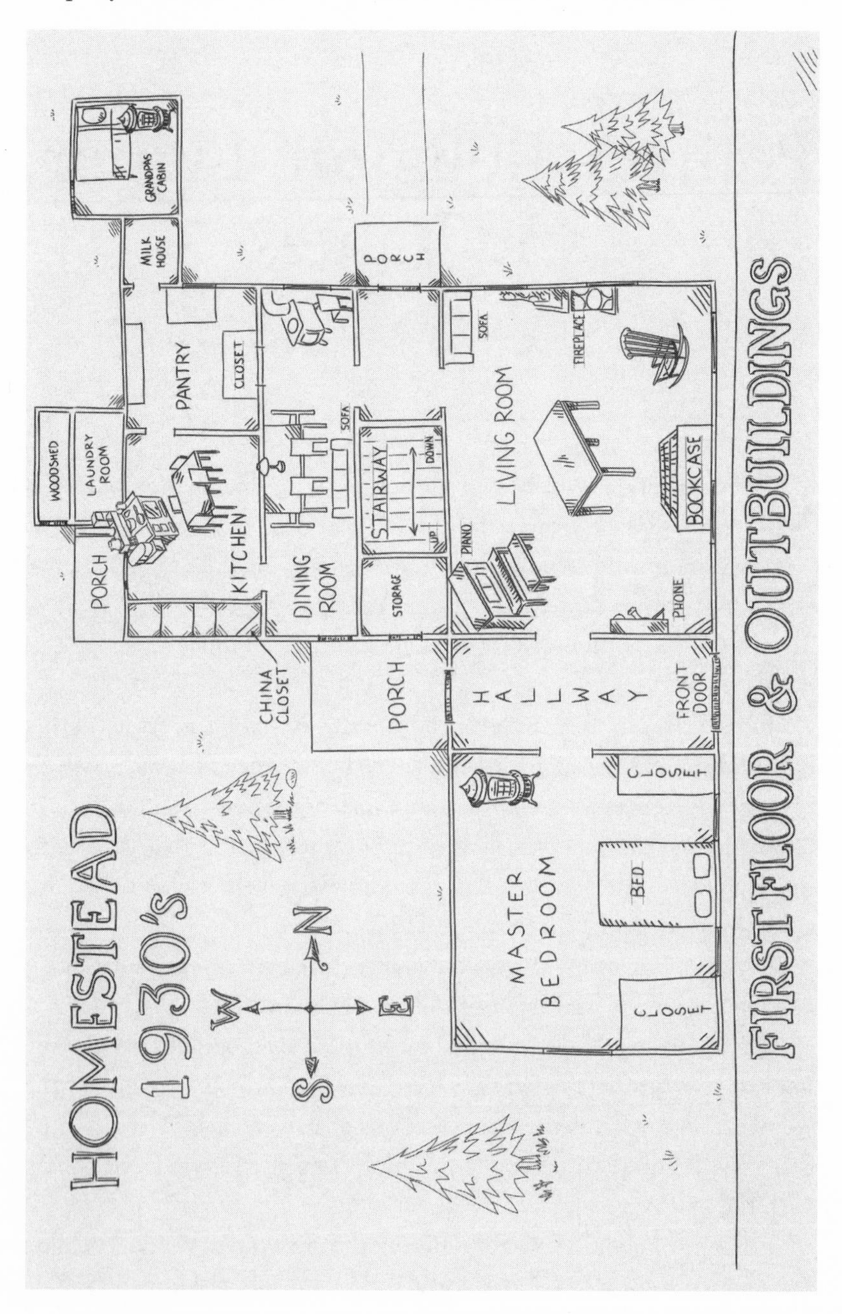

Thomas Dewey, a Republican, came to Bend on his presidential campaign in 1948. He was a little short man with a top hat and mustache and, again, my folks were out in numbers to listen to him. I had met Tom McNellis by then and he was a red-hot Democrat. He would not come to listen to Dewey—said he would not walk across the street to see him! So—again, I kept quiet. I married Tom and my first vote was for Eisenhower—and it took me months to tell Tom. He had a fit. But, over the years, he changed to Republican. Go figure.

I believe Jeannie Jossy, my father's second wife, was Republican, too. But when I visited her in later years after Dad died, I got the feeling that she was a bit more moderate in her views. I just am careful when I am with someone who is very one-way—I have always tried to see good in both parties. Sometimes, that can be hard.

There was no church except in Bend and a place to gather in La Pine. So, my parents' generation had their religious upbringing from my grandmother, Sadie. She taught them well. I believe they said prayers every day and at meals. I think my Aunt Kathryn Grace's diaries show this. I have not read Sadie's diaries for some time, but I know she was very much a church-going girl with her family in Kentucky. That was a given. My brother Claude said that Dad mentioned it when on his deathbed in Bend—about our grandparents' religion and how important it was to them.

We did not go to church—it was just too far to drive in those days. But my Mother wrote that "they" (not sure who) held a Sunday-school class at the ranch regularly and she missed it if the weather was bad. That had to have been in the 1920–1930s era—I have no memory of it. But my Mother played the piano (the one on the ranch now) and just about every week she would play hymns and I would sing them. It was just something we both enjoyed. I have never forgotten those times and I always remembered how to sing those hymns. Sometimes Mother was able to go to a group of women in La Pine where they had a short service and then visited. When I lived in Bend and went to school, I attended about seven or eight of the local churches. I never had a favorite, but loved the Catholic Church for the beauty inside.

On Sundays, when I was growing up, we just did not work outside, except to do necessary chores like milking and carrying water. It was just an easy day—usually with family coming by. My Aunt Mittye came to stay with us after Mother died and she was taken aback that we played board games on Sunday. She was a graduate of a couple of religious schools in the South. But we soon brought her around to our way and she joined us. She was a gem!

The liquor for the dances by the swimming hole at the north end of the ranch most likely came from Bend. There were a lot of the Shevlin people that came to the dances and they shopped in Bend on the weekends. I do not know if there was a liquor store in the lumber camp or not—I doubt it. In later years, I think La Pine had a liquor store, but that was long after the dances were done. Also in later years, the 1930s and 1940s, my family went to dances at the La Pine Grange Hall (still there) and anyone having liquor on their breath was asked to leave. It was a family night. I did see some interesting incidents there when someone would be asked to leave—usually a logger who was single.

As for Prohibition (from 1920 to 1933), I have no idea what people did. I am sure that there was a lot of very bad beer and liquor made from whatever they had to work with (I am speaking of the public). It took me moving to Gig Harbor to find local fishermen that made awful-tasting beer (I thought). There were three bachelor brothers who were our neighbors and who drank every day. That was in the 1950s and 1960s. They also made "white lightning." I tasted it just once and that was enough!

We did not have any liquor in our home, except for "medicinal purposes." That was brandy for me when I had the "croup" as a child. Dad would wet a teaspoon full of sugar with the brandy and I would swallow it (loved the taste!). It would stop my coughing for awhile. He would sit with me in front of the fireplace and rock me and it is something I can never forget.

In the same 1932 letter I mentioned earlier, my mother said, "Our state went wet, but we were very sorry. Maybe the people will tire of it soon...." The "wets" were the people who wanted to allow the sale of alcohol and the "drys" were the people who did not.

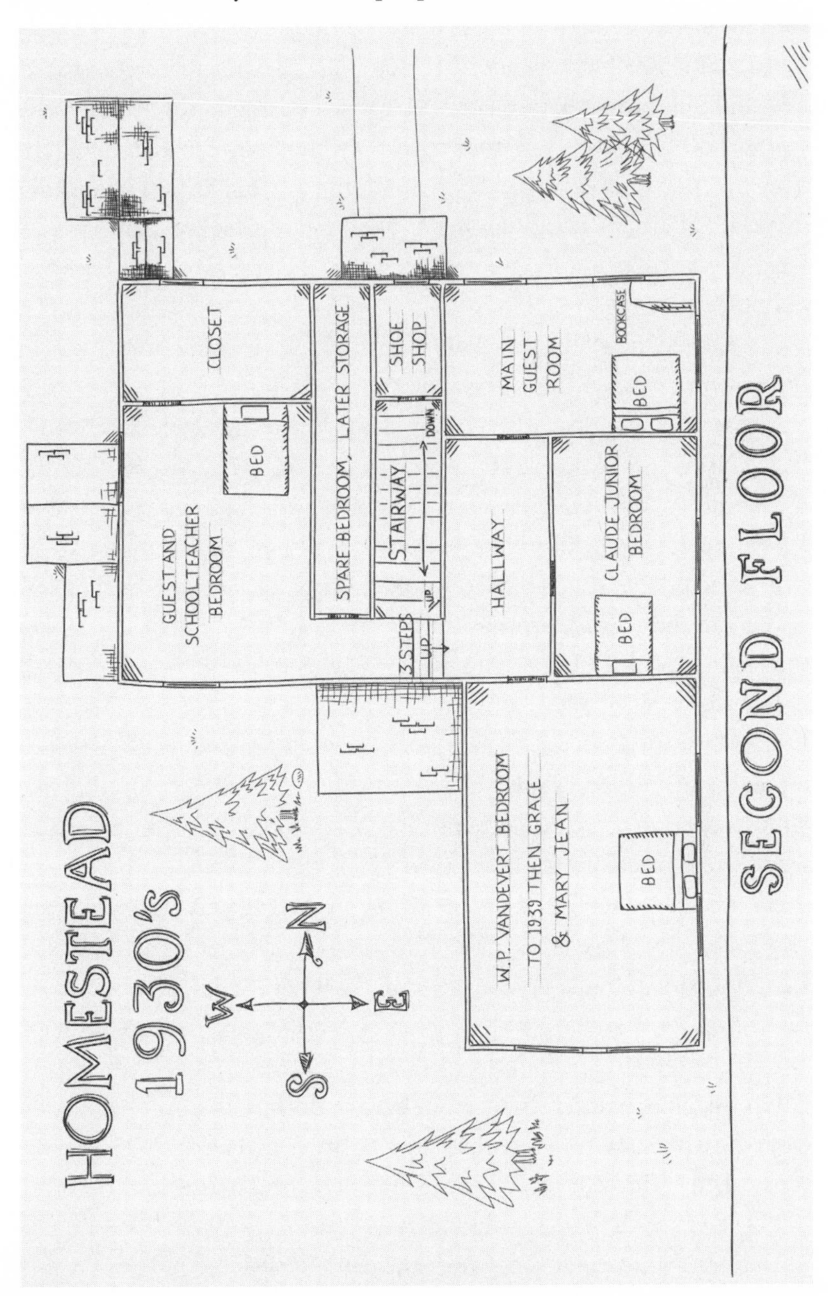

My parents, Claude and Pearl, simply did not drink. We had a couple come maybe twice a year to the ranch for a few days and they were used to having a cocktail before dinner every day. My Mother had to hide her feelings about it—she just did not understand it at all—but she loved them dearly. So every evening before dinner, the couple had a drink—I am not sure if they knew my Mother's feelings. She was not a "goody-goody"—but I can remember always asking my Dad whether I could tell her a joke I heard at school. That would have been when I was about nine years old and going to La Pine Schools.

I believe Uncle Bill and Aunt Dorothy felt the same way. I was in their home so many times and never, ever saw liquor.

As for the doctors and their families, I know my Uncle Doc would have a drink—he belonged to several organizations during his lifetime in Bend. My Aunt Harriet entertained her card clubs at her home, but I have no idea if drinks were served. I did know that some of those ladies, including Aunt Harriet, smoked. My mother thought that was wrong. So did Aunt Dorothy. I never saw Uncle George or Uncle Arthur take a drink, but my brother Dave says they would have a cocktail before dinner.

As for our Grampa—every year he received beautiful bottles of liquor from his old cronies at the courthouse in Bend. He did like wine and he kept it stashed upstairs in his room. The empty bottles went into a piece of furniture called a hall tree. We would clean it out every so often—actually a couple times a year. He only drank it when he went to bed. I never ever saw him with it. I still have that hall tree. I am not sure of Sadie's feelings—but I will bet she had none of it. As for selling it—I doubt it very much. Even if Grampa had wanted to, I am sure Sadie put her foot down.

In his later years, I know my Dad would have a beer if someone came by with some. Also, Jeannie and I always had a cocktail when we went to the Mexican restaurant in Sunriver. She loved that! So did I but we were both pretty straight arrows.

So—it sounds like they were all teetotalers—sort of—but it just simply was not part of our life. It just was not around for us to even try. I had my first drink at 18 years old.

My family lived good and wholesome lives, but we did not think we were special because of it. It just seemed natural to be honest, work hard in school and on the ranch, and be friendly to other people. We did not have any code to live by. It was just the way you acted.

None of us were rebellious when we were kids. I think we knew our parents loved us and were always looking out for us. We knew we were lucky. Of course, we did not have many of the temptations kids have today. We did not know anybody who broke the law or kept getting in trouble. We listened to the same radio programs and music our parents did. There were no drugs around—we did not even know about them.

I also think having so many different animals on the ranch gave us a kind of perspective on life. They each had their own quirks—things they liked or did not like or were afraid of. And they all depended on us to take care of them one way or another. I have read that taking care of animals can be great therapy for mixed-up teenagers and I can certainly understand that. I do not think any of us had any real difficulties but maybe the animals helped make sure that we did not.

I am lucky that my five sons all turned out well and it looks like my grandchildren will too. But sometimes I wish they could grow up on the ranch like I did. I think they would have enjoyed it a lot and they would not have to deal with some of the bad things in life so early.

CHAPTER 13

Third Generation

In the fall of 1942, Claude and Pearl were expecting a child, due in January 1943. Pearl did not feel well for a few days and fell into a half-conscious state late one night. Claude called his brother, Clint, the doctor in Bend, and started the generator to get the lights going.

Pearl kept asking for Grace, her 13-year-old daughter, but did not recognize that Grace was right next to her. Grace rubbed her arms when Pearl said she felt numb. As soon as Clint arrived, he called for an ambulance. Pearl died two days later in the hospital in Bend. Her son, Dave, was born on November 3, 1942, the day before Pearl died. Dave survived undamaged in spite of being born two months early in a time when the science of caring for premature babies was not well understood.

Pearl's death was a catastrophe for her entire family. She was the great love and companion of her husband's life. Not only did he miss her terribly, he had four children needing their mother, including two young girls and a brand-new baby. Claude Junior had just started his freshman year at Oregon State but had to give up college to meet his family's needs for emotional support and work on the ranch. Grace was deeply attached to her mother and refused for a week to believe she was gone. She still misses her mother 70 years later. Mary Jean was only eight when her mother died, a tender age for such a rude shock. Dave, of course, never got to know his mother at all.

The family brought Dave home from the hospital when he was three months old in February 1943. Claude Senior's oldest sister, Mittye, came to the ranch to care for Dave while Claude Senior drove Grace and Mary Jean into Bend every day for school. That first summer of 1943, Claude Junior camped out, alone with the cattle, at Sparks Lake, over 20 miles from the ranch. Claude had a tent at the lake and lived there during the week with the cattle. He had to tie his meat up in the trees to keep animals from getting to it. Grace says,

> "For the school year of 1943–1944, a year after our mother died, we lived on Dekalb Avenue in Bend. Dad took a job with a local trucking firm that delivered around Bend and we were all home at night together. The war was on and we had sold our cattle. When Dad went back to the ranch, I stayed on with the folks that rented the house to us—they were friends of the family—and continued to go to Bend High School as a freshman. My brother Claude also studied at Bend High School, even though he had already graduated. He volunteered for all the armed services but none would take him because of his eyes.
>
> "We found other families to care for Dave. In 1943–1944, we took him to Portland to my mother's niece who had just adopted a little boy. The next winter (1944-1945), Dave, Mary Jean, and I stayed with a good friend on Drake Road in Bend, whose husband was overseas. She had two little girls of her own. It was just across the Newport Bridge. My Aunt Dorothy and Uncle Bill took Dave for the next two winters. We brought Dave home to be with us every summer. He was a great little boy and we all loved him so much.
>
> "I wanted to quit school to care for Dave, but Dad wouldn't let me. He said education was too important. During the summers that we had Dave, we kept very busy. We still had family coming from Portland to visit the ranch and stay a week or so—and the haying went on. We hired a lady one summer to help Dad so that he could be free to do things he needed to do. Then, when Dave was five—the winter after I graduated from high school in 1947—Dad kept him home on the ranch during the school year."

Aunt Mittye rented a room from a family named Organ that was related to the Niswonger family that had been in Bend for many years. The Organs had moved to Bend from Wisconsin where their daughter, Nancy, had grown up. Grace says, "Aunt Mittye thought Nancy would be an ideal girl for my brother Claude. Nancy was working for a local optometrist on Wall Street and walked right by the Ward Automobile Company where Claude was working every day. He had seen her and wondered about her. Aunt Mittye arranged for them to meet. They married in Bend March 21, 1948, and were still married 62 years later when this book was written. They have three children, Claude III, Sue, and Bill. It appears that Aunt Mittye, spinster though she was, knew what she was doing.

Nancy Organ's family lived next to a lady named Kate Rockwell, known widely as "Klondike Kate." Kate grew up in a mansion in Spokane but achieved fame as a flirtatious dancer and vaudeville star during the Alaskan gold rush in 1899. She ran a theater in Seattle and, like many others, tried homesteading on land east of Bend without much luck. She trained starlets in Hollywood before moving back to Bend and next to the Organ family in 1947. The family referred to her as "Aunt Kate." Grace met her and says about her, "She was fun to be around. She wore all colors of clothing—large hats with feathers, carried a cane, and wore long dresses—with maybe a fur stole around her neck. She had been, and maybe still was, wealthy. My cousin Joan (Dr. Clint Vandevert's daughter) said that Aunt Kate used to baby-sit her and Jack when they were small. She had a big heart and always took care of anyone that was needy. My folks had a lot of respect for her. Kate and her husband eventually moved to the Willamette Valley.

About the time he married Nancy, Claude Junior started working for Leonard Lundgren at the Lelco Mill and Lumber Company. Lelco used a portable sawmill that they moved about every two months. Claude worked in the mill, skidded logs to the mill, and built roads. The company worked near Bachelor Butte and a bit south of it for a while. Claude became the boss of the operation when the mill was moved to the Warm Springs Indian Reservation. Claude drove his crew from Bend to the forest everyday in what was called a "crummy." The crummy was a GMC one-ton panel truck that could hold up to 12 men. It had a seat across the back that would hold four men, and then two more seats going forward behind the driver.

In 1961, Claude and Nancy moved to Portland where Claude started working for Tektronix, a company headquartered in Beaverton that became a world leader in test, measurement and monitoring technology. The first six years, he was a bench calibrator of instruments, a job he had studied hard to get. Then he went into management and supervised 18 to 40 people for the next 16 years. He retired in 1983.

Grace attended Bend High School for eighth grade through twelfth, from September 1942 to graduation in 1947.

"For two years, I lived with a family on Drake Road because there was no school bus from the ranch and it was too far for Dad to drive every day. One year, David and Mary Jean lived in the same house with me. In my senior year, I lived separately with a family on Drake Road and worked for my room and board. The couple owned the local bowling alley and needed to be gone in the evenings. I took care of their little girl. Drake Road had some really nice homes in those days. Tom Brooks and his family lived there. They owned the Brooks-Scanlon Mill. My Uncle George and his family lived there for several years in the late 1920s and that house is still there.

"The war was on while I was at Bend High in my eighth through tenth grade, so we said goodbye to some of the senior boys who joined the service. It was a rare time. When I turned 15, my Dad gave me permission to donate blood to the war cause. I did this once a month, I believe, and felt very good about it. They had a place to do this on Wall Street and I think they had a building set aside to handle it. I felt very patriotic!

"The Bend High School building is still there—and is just across Wall Street from the new library that was built in about 2001. The building goes all the way through to Bond Street and is a two story building with lots of stone work. The next large building to the south was our gymnasium and is now a recreational building of some kind. It was built many years ago and still stands. Then, just to the south of that building is the Des Chutes Historical Museum, which was the Reid Elementary School where my sister Mary Jean went.

"Those three buildings are all beside each other. Claude would pick me up at the high school on the Bond Street side and then we would pick up Mary Jean at the Reid School next door. It worked out well.

"During the school year, we had football season in the fall and basketball in the winter time. The high school football games were always on Friday nights. The field was located close to Third Street and Franklin Avenue. The railroad tracks ran around the south end and west side of the field. There were no other buildings in that area except on Third street so there was lots of room for parking and the field. We had two large grandstands—one on either side of the field.

"We usually walked to the game as no one had cars. But Bend was a lot smaller then. The students walked everywhere and were used to it. It was the same for the basketball games held at the old gym next to the high school

"It was always cold by the time the football games were over, so we wore warm clothing. Girls didn't wear slacks in those days—we wore bobby sox and saddle shoes—so sometimes we remembered to bring blankets for warmth.

"After the games, both football and basketball, we walked downtown to Oregon Avenue where there was an ice cream store called Kessler's. We would gather for an hour or so and then start for home. By that time, it would be 10:30 or 11:00 and it was even colder outside.

"When we were kids at both La Pine and Bend schools, we always stayed with a friend after school if there was to be a game played—then the folks would come to the game and we would go home together afterwards. That stopped after our Mother died in 1942.

"When I was 15 and a sophomore, the school district gave me a car. It was because they couldn't afford to have the Bend School district send a bus out to pick us up and take us home every day. So I had a special license and drove the 1940 Chevrolet four-door car with my sister to school in Bend. The gear shift was on the steering wheel, which I thought was wonderful, not on the floor. It was a very good car. After I graduated, Dad had the car and I think Claude bought it from the school district and used it for a few years.

"Also, when we had a car to use after the games, we would go out Highway 97 approximately across from the Hong Kong Restaurant that is still there now, at the corner of Third and Wilson, to a drive-in called The Skyline Drive-In. The Skyline was a small white building with lots of windows and lots of parking space. They had marvelous milkshakes and hamburgers. We would go in to order and sometimes eat in the small booths and have a great time discussing the latest. But lots of times, we took our hamburgers and drove around with whoever had a car. That was great fun. Our cars would be loaded with kids, so, somehow, we drove carefully and never got in trouble. We were very lucky kids.

"Since I had a car a lot of the time, I drove to the Friday games and then drove back to the ranch after going to Kessler's or the Youth Club we had called 'The Bear's Den' right across the street from Kessler's. I would drive home after delivering my girlfriends home. I always drove home in the time that was allotted to me by Dad and I never gave him reason to worry. I just couldn't do that. He gave me a lot of room to grow up in those days.

"Once in a while, I would stay overnight with a friend and then drive home on Saturday morning to the ranch. If I stayed in Bend overnight, I usually did some grocery shopping on Saturday and then left for the ranch. There were always chores waiting at home and Dad was by himself. He was so very good to me about all those things. I never thought to do anything he would disapprove of.

"It was when I returned to my 25th graduation reunion that I found out how lucky I was to have a car in those days. The boys were totally enthralled with the idea that I could drive whenever I wanted and they didn't even own a car. Gas was rationed and it was hard times.

"I once managed to wreck the 1940 car—went off the icy road on the way to school right where the Sunriver exit is. While getting it fixed, Dad made me drive in his car every day so I wouldn't be scared to do it. What a guy! It was the 1941 Chevy two-door that he bought used in 1941 and it was special when I got to drive it to school. Unlike the 1940 Chevy, it had a radio! So, when I got to drive Dad's car, I was in heaven. I was a music nut in those days. The radio was for listening to all the latest hit songs and to know all the words. My sis and I loved that.

"When it got to be cold and snowy, we moved into Bend to a friend's home and stayed until the weather changed."

Grace met her husband-to-be, Tom McNellis, exactly one day after her eighteenth birthday. He was originally from Philadelphia and had found his way to Bend. He worked at the Fall River Fish Hatchery and then for Pacific Power and Light. Mary Jean tells a story about Tom visiting the ranch:

Tom McNellis at the Fall River Fish Hatchery, before he and Grace were married.

"One time, during duck and goose hunting season, Tom McNellis came to the ranch as he had a few times before. He eagerly took off by himself along the river, shotgun in hand. Pop was working around outside the house and I was following him around as usual. We heard a shout and looked up. Here comes Tom trotting, almost running, toward the house, with a huge grin on his face and holding up a large white bird. He was so proud.

"Look at what I've got. A goose and look at the size of it!" Well, Pop did look at the size of it and he may have gone a little pale himself. He dropped his ax or shovel or whatever and, as Tom got closer, Pop's suspicions were confirmed.

"Tom, that is not a goose—it's a swan!" This happened in the late 1940s or early 1950s and, though the spotted owl problem hadn't been spotted yet, there were limits. The limit on swans was zero. What's more, the fine for killing a swan was $500. In those days that was many people's yearly income. To make matters worse, we looked up and could see dust on the road heading our way. It was the local woodcutter who lived a couple of miles away. Pop started running towards Tom, yelling at him (and my Dad was not a yeller). "Tom, Tom, we have got to hide that thing right now." Tom looked, as Pop would say, confounded, wondering what was going on when he'd just made one of his best bird hunting conquests.

"They hid it in the woodshed until the woodcutter finished his conversation. When he was gone, they took it across the river and buried it deep in the woods and deeply in the ground, where it would not be found by wild animals and dug up with white feathers strewn all over. I believe it is understandable that Pop didn't turn Tom into the sheriff. I believe even more that Tom was happy about that, too."

Tom was a Catholic and Grace was not. When wedding plans started to get complicated, Tom and Grace went to Klamath Falls on their own and returned man and wife in February 1950. For a while, they lived with Uncle Bill and Aunt Dorothy. Uncle Bill was recovering from surgery at the time and they helped take care of him. The first of the couple's five sons, Tom, was born in April of 1951 while they were living on Ogden Street in Bend. Uncle Doc delivered the boy with the help of a nurse Grace had known since she was a little girl.

The couple decided to move to Philadelphia and Tom went ahead to find a job. The airlines were on strike so Grace followed by train. Grace bravely left Central Oregon behind and saw the country out the train window with her new baby. Tom worked for Leeds and Northrup, a company that built manufacturing controls, and Grace worked for the Home Insurance Company, right across from Independence Hall. Tom and Grace's second son, Mike, was born in September of 1952 at Temple University Hospital in Philadelphia.

In 1953, with two sons in tow, Tom and Grace drove across the country back to Bend. Grace says she knows how her ancestors felt going west. She was never so glad to see a place as she was to see Pilot Butte. Within two weeks the couple had moved on to Gig Harbor, Washington. They bought a house in 1955 and brought up their family, including three more sons who were born there—John, Steve, and Joe. Grace still lives in Gig Harbor and all of her sons live in the area.

Grace remembers her sister, Mary Jean, as a baby—a beautiful redhead, very sweet and always a joy. Born in 1934, Mary Jean helped Grace raise their little brother David, born in 1942. The girls always managed to keep David happy when they had him under their wing. David and Mary Jean remained very close in their adulthood.

Mary Jean delighted in the ranch and wrote, later in life, about the sights, smells, and everything else connected with it. She started first grade at Reid School in Bend and graduated from Bend High School in 1953. She lived in Philadelphia for one year with Grace and Grace's new family. Mary Jean, often simply called Mary, helped look after Grace's two boys and they loved her. She visited many historical sites and worked in downtown Philadelphia.

Mary Jean had already met her future husband, Jack Organ, who was a brother of Nancy Organ, Claude Junior's wife. After Jack and Mary Jean were married, they lived in Seattle. Jack worked for Boeing as a tool and die maker. Their two children, Dan and Mitti, were born there. The family moved to San Diego and then back to Portland.

Mary Jean was an avid basketball fan. She kept individual score sheets for the Portland Trailblazers and watched every game. Her favorite players were Clyde "The Glide" Drexler, Buck Williams, and Terry Porter. She knew them all and could always tell people their stats.

She was a very religious lady and worked with her church in every way she could. She was always there to lend a hand and people loved her for it. Mary Jean died on March 13, 2003, at St. Vincent's Hospital in Portland.

Mary Jean's affection for the ranch comes through in excerpts from the monograph she wrote in 1991:

> "The clear blue sky with its fluffy white clouds is one of the first things you notice when coming over the mountains from the Willamette Valley. I remember it mostly during the hot summer days when playing outside or swimming in the Little Deschutes, or during the haying season because, usually, it was *HOT*. I loved it when I had the river to jump into or when I was lying on a blanket in the shade. Out in the sun, when everyone else was getting a tan, I was getting a sunburn and freckles. But the beauty of the sky was undeniable.
>
> "The night sky, black as black can be, was filled with a million twinkling stars, and the moon, sometimes a silver wisp and some-

times huge and golden, rising in the east behind the silhouette of the jack pine trees. Watching those stars when lying in the cool evening grass, we did not need to say anything at all. My favorite summers (nearly every one) were when Pop would put out, right by the old house's dining room porch or off the front porch, an old rusty pair of bedsprings, an old mattress and bedding complete with a full-length tarp to cover it during rainstorms. Then you could lie there and try to count the stars until you went to sleep. You didn't need a cassette tape of the ocean or a bubbling brook with frogs and night sounds—you had it right there, with the river only 40 feet from the house. Another beautiful sight was the summer nights when the aurora borealis would glow pink, red, white, and sometimes a shade of green, rising and falling like a colorful cascading waterfall. Sometimes we could look up and see the colors all around us.

"Sunsets were sensational. Every one was different. Sometimes the colors were covering the whole sky in pinks and lavenders. Sometimes they were only behind the mountains and the hills where the colors might be reds and fiery golds, then gradually fading to the softer colors. To take it all in, we would walk up to the rock pile by the front gate, where you could see all of the mountains. I must admit that some of the sunsets at the coast are just as beautiful, but nothing quite matches the complete picture at the ranch with the mountains, forests, willows, river, fields, and especially watching the cattle and horses and, usually, deer grazing as the sun finally went down."

Grace and Mary Jean remembered growing up on the ranch very fondly. They had great parents and an older brother who was very good to them. But their brother Claude Junior was a bit more eager to put the past behind him. He worked very hard without having a stake in the ranch himself. He was an excellent student but did not get to put his mental skills to use until much later in life. He had just started his college education when he needed to return to the ranch after his mother died.

David Vandevert was the last member of the family to grow up on the ranch. David's story will be told in a later chapter about the 1950s and 1960s.

CHAPTER 14

Town of Harper and Harper School

When kayakers and canoeists pull their boats out of the Deschutes River at the Harper Bridge on Spring River Road, some must wonder where the name Harper came from. Who was Harper? A long-forgotten governor of Oregon? The engineer who built the bridge? Perhaps a highway department supervisor in the 1940s? In fact, Harper was a town. Harper was located on the southeast corner of South Century Drive and Spring River Road. Harper is long gone and the site is now occupied by a power station and parts of the Caldera Springs practice golf course.

In 1971, Claude Vandevert Senior wrote, "David Hill was a homesteader here in 1906 and 1907 when the railroad survey came through. He got the idea of a town which he named Harper. It never grew much, but they did sell quite a few lots and had a hotel and a store." The railroad between Bend and Chemult was not built until 1928, over 20 years after the survey. But what killed Harper in the meantime was not the delayed arrival of the railroad. It was the sudden arrival of the automobile.

Leona Stocking was the granddaughter of the one-time owner of the Harper Hotel, Peter Thompson. Stocking wrote a history of her grandfather's family that found its way to the Crook County Historical Society:

"The Harper Hotel was situated about halfway between Bend and La Pine, Oregon. The location, which had previously been called Lava, was designed to become a town and there were survey stakes all around. The road had a bend to the east just here and the hotel faced this road, facing to the west. It was a very important hotel, necessary as a stopping and change-over place on the stage route between Bend and La Pine. The run continued to Klamath Falls. The stage from La Pine arrived about eleven o'clock in the morning for a change of horses. The passengers and driver would have their dinner at the hotel. They would just get on their way when the coach from Bend would arrive about two o'clock in the afternoon. Each coach used a four horse hook-up.

"Peter Thompson from Minnesota arrived here in January 1916, looking for a place to buy that would have jobs for his growing family. The hotel seemed ideal as there would be cooking, waiting on tables, cleaning of rooms, etc. for his wife and girls. He and his sons would handle the stable and change of horses. There was also a small store in a front room of the hotel.

"Peter made a deal with Marion Miller to buy the hotel. The Millers were a settled family in the area. Marion and his wife owned and operated the Harper Hotel. Marion's brother homesteaded about a half a mile to the southeast."

Perhaps this is where the remains of a log cabin are today in the golf course at Caldera Springs. Stocking continues in her history:

"Peter was born in Glenwood, Minnesota. His wife, Signe, arrived there from Norway as a young woman. They married and proceeded to have 10 healthy children, even though they moved back and forth to Montana a couple of times during those years.

"Peter returned to the family in Donaldson, Minnesota, and had a farm sale on February 26, 1916. The family was all elated as they boarded the train for Bend. They eagerly settled into the hotel. It seemed like a big place to the children, though the building was only about 22 feet wide and about 40 feet long. It was built of lumber, wide boards of yellow pine; with a square store-type front, and had two front doors. The door on the south side was the entrance to the small store and office. The other door entered on a sitting room which had a stairway to the second floor. A large dining room spread across the width of the house just behind these two rooms. In the back were a bedroom and a kitchen with an access door into a lean-to woodshed. There were nine bedrooms upstairs. The floors throughout the hotel were boards.

"The soil was sandy around the hotel but there was one damp spot where water almost came out of the ground. Peter dug a well there, not far from the hotel. He set an open-ended barrel in the hole for a casing. It made a very shallow well but there was lots of water.

"The barn was a short distance to the south of the hotel, probably about 28 by 40 feet. They kept a complete change of horses there for the stagecoach. There was a small school about 300 yards east of the hotel."

This preceded the "Harper School" building that was built in 1925 and moved to Vandevert Ranch in 1929. Stocking continues:

"For the start of school in September, Peter Thompson was instrumental in finding a teacher who boarded at the hotel and taught eight children. Miss Brinks had a brother in Bend who was a lawyer and she went there for most of her weekends. Miss Ransom replaced her in the spring.

"Mr. Frederick L. Rice came to teach at the school in September of 1917. (School records indicate he came in October 1916.) He boarded at the hotel and went to his home in Bend on the weekends. He always chewed on raisins. He must have bought them by the pound.

"A traveling minister stopped at the hotel and managed to arrange to borrow Peter's Ford car. He kept it for about two weeks and Peter was getting a bit upset. He really got upset when the man at the garage in Bend got in touch with him to say that the minister had brought the car in for repair and it would cost him 35 dollars to get it out of the garage. It was a major rear-end job and it was a lot of money at that time. Peter was always a bit leery about ministers after that.

"The family drove to the town of Bend in the Ford touring car to do their shopping. They stopped on the way one day and all climbed

Lava Butte. There were pine trees growing all over the north side of the butte with a few more right up on the top. The crater was a fascinating sight. There was a regular type telephone booth situated at the top, kept locked, with a telephone inside. The fire ranger would climb the butte and check periodically for fires around. There was a lot of valuable timber in sight, mostly yellow pine and jack pine.

"The Canada geese wintered on the Deschutes River, a small flock of perhaps 50. One day Peter crept up on them and was able to shoot three geese with his 12-gauge single barrel shotgun before they flew away. The family enjoyed them for their Christmas dinner in 1917. They made a very nice change.

"Cars and trucks were beginning to move around more freely and the stagecoach was losing both freight and passengers. It was hard to make ends meet and Peter went to work in the logging camp. Arnold, Peter and Signe's son, got a part time job on the log landing near home as they prepared the logs for floating down the river toward Bend."The log landing was where the Spring River Bridge is today or just north of it."

Leona Stocking then mentions other neighbors, including the Vandeverts:

"Another of their neighbors was the Vandevert family, living about two miles south of the hotel. One of the sons became a doctor and when Palmer (one of Peter and Signe's sons) had a heart attack, Dr. Vandevert was called.

"A new teacher, Miss Arnold, came to teach at the Harper School in the spring of 1918. She was a young lady and very pretty. She also boarded at the hotel.

"Peter and Signe realized they had bought the hotel at a bad time. The stagecoach run was discontinued. Trucks and cars had completely taken the business away. So Peter made a deal with Mike Mayfield who had a ranch over on the Crooked River south of Prineville (now the Prineville reservoir). Mike needed someone to put up the hay on the ranch for his cattle herd in the winter. There was a nice ranch house there so Peter took five of the children over there to put up the hay.

"When September of 1918 came, Miss Ransom returned to teach but she had married in the interval and was now Mrs. Royer. Two Thompson children (Selma and Arnold) went to Bend for high school and rented one end of a long, narrow house from Mr. Metke who lived in the other end. It was about a block from the high school. Peter let Arnold use the model-T one ton truck to drive to school for the week. It had solid rubber tires and a flat deck on the back. The young people were able to go home on the weekend or sometimes Arnold would take part of the basketball team to Redmond or Prineville to play basketball. Signe was alone with the younger children at the hotel much of the time and Arnold would phone her and bring the necessary groceries home.

"Henry went to work at Lava Butte. A camp had set up for a crew to haul cinders on the road. They were extremely dusty with the extra traffic and there was very little rain. Peter and Henry were both waiting to be called up when World War I ended. Tom's regiment was ready to sail for England when they got the news.

"Peter and Signe sold the hotel to a man who never paid them so it was a great loss."

The schoolhouse now on Vandevert Ranch was originally built in 1925 on a low hill just north of the junction of South Century Boulevard and Spring River Road, not far from the Harper Hotel. Anzonetta Caldwell Rupe wrote about the building of the school on the knoll near Harper in 1925 when she was 10 years old.

The Harper School in its original location on a knoll above the corner of South Century and Spring River Road. It was built in 1925 and moved to the ranch in 1929.

"There must not have been any carpenters available or maybe no funds available and everyone concerned seemed to be otherwise fully occupied. Mr. Daly ran a dairy and delivered bottled milk to the Shevlin-Hixon logging camp. Mr. Maker took care of the pump house and pumps that supplied water to the camp, and my father worked as a timber faller six days a week for the camp.

"John Atkinson and his wife had no children, but Mr. Atkinson must have been on the District School Board, or in some influential position, as he seemed to be the one who arranged for the lumber, windows, and the one door, etc., for the new school. I was anxious to get back to school, as I would be in the fourth grade and figured that a great advancement over the third. I didn't pay much attention to the talk of the arrangements to get the building up until my mother announced that she and Gladys Daly would help Mr. Atkinson get it built. As was the way of many pioneer women, my mother was handy with tools such as shovels, axes, hammers, and saws. Mr. Atkinson and his two helpers were soon hard at work. Mrs. Daly brought her three children with her each morning while my sister and I accompanied Mother. We five children played nearby and the building took shape. We brought lunches so everyone spent the entire day and, in only a few days, a small, bright new schoolhouse stood on the knoll. I remember looking up at the roof one day and watching Mother and Mrs. Daly busily nailing on shingles or they may have been shakes. Two little buildings with half-moons in the door stood out back.

"There were only six or eight elementary children so the teacher said she would teach two or three others who were ninth graders, as they had no transportation to high school which was either in La Pine or Bend, about 15 miles either way.

Rupe says, "I think we all enjoyed that year in the little new schoolhouse. In the spring of 1926, the day after school let out, my family left for California and I have never seen the Harper School again."

In 1929, the schoolhouse was moved to the northeast corner of Vandevert Ranch, where it still is today, about a 50 yards west of South Century Drive. The front door, the only door to the school, faces north and there is great view of Mt. Bachelor from the little porch by the door. A road that no longer exists ran east-west in front of the school, down to the Little Deschutes River and across it on a bridge to serve a few families that lived between the Little Deschutes and the Big Deschutes. The school closed in 1937 but reopened again in 1946. The school finally stopped operating 10 years later.

Grace attended the Harper School for first and second grade, from September 1935, when she was six years old, to May 1937. These were Claude's eighth grade and freshman years at the same school. Grace remembers those years well:

> "The school room had windows facing east so that we got the morning sun. The windows were moved to the west side when the school was restored in the 1990s. There were five rows of desks with about three desks across in each row. Claude sat next to the windows and I sat next to the blackboard on the west side of the room. We faced south towards the teacher's desk. There were blackboards on the south and west sides of the room. The stove was on the west side in the rear of the room. On the north side of the room were some shelves and that is where we kept all the library books that were delivered every month or so from Bend.

The restored classroom in the Harper School. When the Vandeverts attended the wood stove was in the near right corner by the entrance.

> "There were several children in school at different times during those two years. Some families came and went when the snow got bad. There were times when it was just Claude and me in school. Claude was the only one in his grades at that time. I had no one in the first grade with me. I was by myself, but didn't mind.

"Claude would be up early on days we went to school on the ranch. He had chores to do outside depending on the time of year. I was allowed to sleep until about seven. By then, the kitchen and dining room were warmed up by the wood stoves and I would dress in a small closet off the room. By the time I was dressed for school, my Dad was back from across the bridge or the barn after milking the two cows. He and my Mother would take care of straining the milk into pans and setting them in the milk-house to cool. Claude would fix our lunch to take to school and then we all sat down to breakfast.

"Claude would leave about 8:00 a.m. to go across the field and open the school up for the day. He did all the janitor work such as starting the stove, splitting wood, pumping water from the well and, most days, sweeping out the room. He brought in wood and a bucket of fresh water for drinking. He had it all ready by the time the rest of the students got to school. The cloak room was where we hung our coats and put our lunches on a shelf. Also, there was a wash-pan and soap and towels for us to use during the day.

"I would be sent walking across the field about a half hour after Claude left. I followed a small trail and sometimes the dogs would follow me, but I sent them home where they should be. The teacher was usually there by the time I arrived and I believe we started school at 9:00. We sometimes adjusted the time due to bad weather.

"Because little girls didn't wear slacks or jeans in those days, we dressed warmly when the cold weather came. We had sweaters and skirts and long socks that we held up with garters from around our waists. Then when it was time to go to school, we had to put on galoshes (I called them over-shoes). They were rubber on the outside and had about four hooks to button up. That kept our shoes dry walking when it was wet with snow.

"I also had to put on a snowsuit of some kind along with hat and mittens. By then, I was bundled almost too much to walk. Now I must tell you that the folks didn't let me walk to school if it were snowing out or we were having a blizzard. Either we had school at the house or waited until the weather got better. Sometimes, Dad would simply put us in the car and take us to school. He would help Claude get the building ready and then go back home.

"Claude would ski to the schoolhouse when there was snow. He kept his skis waxed and he also waxed mine. My pair was much shorter than his—maybe four feet long—and if there was no storm, they let me ski across the field. Again, you should know that I'm quite sure that both of my parents, or at least one, would be watching me all the way. I know Dad would say 'He made it okay' when Claude got to the school and I'm sure they watched me trucking across the field.

"School was out by 3:30 and I would head for home across the field. Sometimes we might just walk on the road back to the house. There were very few cars in those days, but always there were tire tracks to walk in. That made it easy to walk and we usually came home together. Dad could see us whichever way we came.

"There was no playing around either on the way to school or coming home—you knew you had to just keep going! We learned well.

"I loved going home and my Dad was usually there with my Mother. We would listen to a couple of favorite radio shows—15 minutes in length—every weekday. Claude would get home soon after me if he didn't come along at the same time and we both loved those old radio plays.

"We started the school day with the pledge of allegiance. Then the teacher would give Claude an assignment and go to each child and give them something to do. We studied reading, writing, and arithmetic. By the second grade, I studied a bit of history and geography. Claude was into algebra by that time. We wrote our numbers, had penmanship, read Dick and Jane books, and each class would last about 45 minutes. As a first-grader, they had "flash-cards" for both arithmetic and words. It worked well and I learned to read with a passion that I never lost over the years.

"Claude was an avid reader as a youngster. He would take a book outside at lunch time at the school, climb up one of the ponderosa pines and sit on a limb and read a book. I'm not kidding! We once had a picture of him up in the tree, but I don't think I have it any more. He was an "A" student—always was—and never missed a day of school in nine years. He got a certificate every year for his 100% attendance record.

"We had recess both morning and afternoon along with an hour for lunch. At recess, we played outside in the nice weather with a ball and bat, or hide and seek, or whatever we could find to do. At lunch, we ate inside and, in the cold of winter, we would bring a can of Campbell's soup and share it with the teacher. Usually we were the only two in attendance. If the weather got really bad with lots of snow, she came and stayed with us at our home and we held school in front of the fireplace in the living room. This could last for a week or more. The teacher sometimes joined us outside and we would include her or him (we had a Mr. Hunnell in my second year) in our antics.

"This part of our education ended the following year when we went to La Pine for school. Claude needed a larger curriculum for his education in the last three years and he graduated from La Pine when he was only 16 years old. He had taken the fourth and fifth grade together at the ranch and started when he was only five years old. So he was still very young.

"I went from the third grade through the sixth grade at La Pine. I loved every minute of it with all those children to play with. I had wonderful teachers and still have friends to this day that we keep in touch with. From there, I went to Allen School for one year in Bend (where the Safeway Store is on Third Street) and then over to the Bend High School where I went from eighth grade through graduation. That, too, was a wonderful time!

"Claude took some post-graduate classes at Bend High School and eventually started at Oregon State University. He had to give that up when we lost our Mother in 1942 and he came home to stay. He felt he needed to be back with the family and, especially, with Dad. Dad took our Mother's death very, very hard and Claude thought he could be of help. He was so right—we all needed him around!"

David Vandevert, Grace's younger brother, attended the school from 1948 to 1956 and wrote the following from memory:

"The white schoolhouse was located at the north end of our property, where it stands today. From the Old Homestead's dining room north window, we could just barely see it through the trees. A one-room schoolhouse, it actually had a very small room on its northern side (the entranceway) used to hang coats, with a table to put our lunches upon. A propane heater warmed the school on cold days. On the south side of the building was a small storage shed, and to the south of the shed were the two outhouses—one for males, and one for females. A well with a hand pump was located a few yards to the west of the school for drinking water and hand washing. On the east side there was a hand-made teeter-totter and a swing."

"My teacher in the first and third through eighth grades was Mrs. Gladys Halligan. She commuted daily from her home on the south side of Bend. She seldom missed a day, even during severe snowstorms. Mrs. Halligan was a wonderful teacher—she not only taught our academic classes well, but also encouraged arts, crafts and music. In fact, I still have a lamp made with a floral design by pressing copper sheets that I made there. I also participated in a music festival in Sisters where I played a solo on the tonette."

The tonette is a small, plastic, end-blown flute invented in 1938. By 1941, over half of the grammar schools in the United States had adopted the tonette. David continues,

"In the second and third grades, Miss Blanchard was our teacher. She was younger and liked to take us on 'field trips' through the forest or down by the river. As I remember, she quite often missed coming to school, and Dad did not like that; he also said that field trips were a waste of time!

"When I began the first grade, there were about 15 or 16 students, several of them from a large family that lived just north of Camp Abbot. A few were from other locations up the river south of the ranch. Also attending were Linda, Claudia, and Lauren James, who lived about three-quarter mile to the west on the Big Deschutes.

"I practically always rode my bicycle to school, along a cow path through the trees on the eastern edge of our property, or on the main road. Even in winter, I would make 'lariats' from plastic and tie them on my rear wheel for chains. Occasionally, when there were southerly winds, I 'sailed' to school on the crust of the snow. I had anchored a sheet sail on my sled, and I zipped to school in minutes! Returning home was a different story.

"From my second through fifth grades, the number of students decreased each year until 1953–1956 when the only students remaining were myself, Claudia James, and her brother, Lauren, who was two years behind us in grade levels. There was a small eighth grade graduation ceremony for Claudia and myself, probably conducted by Mrs. Clara Buckingham, the Deschutes County Office of Education superintendent. (Although she was very nice, all of the students were scared to death of her—probably because of that long, 'important' title.)

"Like any students, we loved recesses! What an environment it was in which to play all kinds of games. One of our favorite play spots was in a huge dead and rotting pine just to the west of the schoolhouse. It was our "ship at sea." Part of the trunk remained standing, and it was hollowed out with room enough for one of us to stand. This was the 'Captain's' quarters, and through a hole we could see the entire log laid out like a ship in front of us. The log also had hollows in it where we could lay and hide out from the captain. Great fun! We also played a variety of ball games, either in the road to the north of the school or on the school ground.

"One winter—maybe I was in the fourth or fifth grade—snow and ice had covered the teeter-totter and no one would sit or step on it. But Dave the Exception wanted to show everyone how he could walk right up to the center of it. So I did, but when I turned around to go down, I slipped and fell on one of the upright posts where there was a short stub of a branch that had not been trimmed off. I cut my lower lip, and it bled profusely. The teacher immediately called Dad. He packed me in the car and took me to Uncle Doc in Bend where he stitched it up. I still have a scar just below my lip.

"We always had some type of celebration for the major holidays. We would make small holiday items from paper or paper mache, and the teacher always brought us special snacks like cookies, candies or cakes for the events. On my birthday in about 1952, in the early afternoon, an ice cream truck pulled into the school and proceeded to give everyone free ice cream! I was thrilled! How could that happen, especially on my birthday? Thinking about it, I concluded that Dad had arranged the whole thing! At home that afternoon, I told him thank you, but he totally denied having anything to do with it!"

CHAPTER 15

Camp Abbot and Sunriver

Within a month of Pearl Vandevert's death in November 1942, a second event brought major changes to the ranch. The U.S. Army requisitioned 5,500 acres a few miles downstream on both sides of the Deschutes River. The land included the future site of Sunriver Resort and the land around Spring River—where the Vandeverts had been grazing their cattle in the summer. The following summer, in 1943, Claude Vandevert Junior camped out with the cattle at Sparks Lake in the high Cascades. That fall, the family sold the entire herd for the first time since the ranch was founded. The price for cattle was good, the troops needed the meat, and the grazing was suddenly more difficult.

The Army acquired the land to set up the third camp in the United States for training combat engineers to fight in Europe in World War II. The camp was named Camp Abbot in honor of Brigadier General Henry Larcom Abbot. Abbot, then a lieutenant, had camped on the site on September 2, 1855, while searching for a possible railroad route between the Sacramento Valley and the Columbia River.

The Army selected Central Oregon for a number of training camps because there was a lot of vacant land and because it was similar, in some ways, to the land they expected to fight over in France and Germany. The Deschutes was supposed to substitute for the Rhine. The forests may have looked somewhat similar, but the sagebrush and juniper in much of Central Oregon certainly did not. It seems the Army thought the troops needed to know how to operate in cold winters. Also, the clear skies year-round allowed the bomber and fighter pilots to get plenty of practice supporting the troops.

Camp Abbot trainees started arriving in March 1943 and the population of the area exploded from a few hundred people to over 10,000. In 1944, Claude Senior found work at the camp that he said paid better than raising cattle.

The camp trained 90,000 individuals, 10,000 at a time. A training cycle lasted 17 weeks with six weeks of general instruction, six weeks of techniques and tactics or specialist training, and three weeks of field maneuvers. The engineers were taught to build bridges and blow them up, to lay minefields, to get through the enemy's minefields, and to build roads and canals.

A special "Oregon Maneuver" took place over three counties in September and October 1943. It involved 100,000 soldiers under the command of Major General Alexander Patch. The engineers built a long bridge over the Deschutes, upriver from Camp Abbot, and named it the General Patch Bridge. Grace recalls,

> "We could hear them when they were practicing artillery. They had a range where they shot due west across the Big Deschutes into the area where we had ranged our cattle. In later years, we found trees torn up from bullets and there were a lot of holes in the ground from where the artillery shells landed.
>
> "Where the Allen ranch was (now the Crosswater Club) the Army built an airfield where we could watch some of the activity. During the war, we were "airplane spotters" and any plane that went over the ranch, we would call a place in Redmond and report that the plane was coming from a certain direction and what its configuration was, and color if possible, and we felt we were contributing to the national safety.
>
> "When the Army maneuvers were in the ranch area, they were all over the place from our property line east to Highway 97—up and down the road from us. It was a huge operation with big Army

trucks going by regularly carrying men. You would see a tank once in awhile going up the road. They actually had tank chases where one tank would chase another.

"Dad visited some of the camps that were set up outside the ranch. These were camps for Army units on maneuvers, not for the engineers at Camp Abbot. One camp was just to the north of what is now Vandevert Road—about half way out to Highway 97. Dad pulled in there one day and saw soldiers burying food of all kinds. There was bread, cheese, and other things. He asked them why they were doing that. One of the soldiers said they did that each time a new batch of soldiers came to the area for a three or four week stay. He said that if they didn't bury what was left from the previous group, they couldn't get enough supplies to last through the next bunch! Dad had a fit. He said, 'If you will let me come and pick it up, I'll see that it gets used.' There was so much rationing going on then.

"So, when Dad found out that he could just take the truck out and they would pile food on it, and that it would continue, he decided to buy some pigs. We built a pen for them across the big bridge (on the west bank of the river) about 150 feet south of the house. It was a large pen—about 150' x 75'—and he bought about 40 'weaner pigs.' These were pigs that had been weaned but still weighed less than 40 pounds. Coyotes never bothered them—we never lost any. The weaner pigs were big enough to look after themselves but too immature to have piglets.

"Then, about three times a week, Dad would simply drive our truck out and the men would load on these 50-gallon barrels of left-over food—straight from the stove—and we took it back to the ranch and dumped it into troughs for the pigs.

"We did that all summer and those pigs gained like mad. Dad said that he thought those pigs ate better than some folks in Bend due to the rationing. The soldiers gave Dad the cheese, bread, and cans of Spam—and we distributed it in Bend to people that needed it. Otherwise, it would have just been buried. I don't remember when these maneuvers stopped, but when they left the area, we sold the pigs locally.

"The bread came in huge paper sacks—about four feet high. They held several loaves of round bread that had a hard crust—and the bread was delicious. We used it ourselves and gave a lot away—especially if the pigs were already fed.

"Not only did the soldiers give Dad the food from the meals right off the stoves—but also fresh meat that otherwise would have been buried. Dad got a couple of lockers in Bend and rescued some of that meat so he could share it with others. Sometimes the soldiers would get to the camp a bit early and there were no supplies in yet. So they had to eat K-rations, which were miserable. I took a taste one time and it was like eating sawdust.

"The soldiers were not allowed to come on the ranch. Our fences all had signs that said 'No Military Personnel Allowed.' Lots of soldiers would hang across the fence when we working and just watch. My Dad would ask if they would like to come in and go down to the river. They loved that. There would be a half dozen soldiers sitting on our big bridge. Dad would fix them fishing poles from willow branches and give them lines and hooks. He said he remembered being so homesick when he was in the Army, during the First World War, that he would have given anything to have someone invite him to their home. One time, there were three African-American soldiers who asked if they could please ride our horses. Dad said that they weren't for 'riding'—they were our work horses. But they kept saying they really wanted to ride them, so Dad made rope halters for our old team and let the men ride around in the upper field. They loved it.

"I remember in the fall after haying, when the nights were getting colder, I invited some soldiers to fill bags with leftover hay from the fields to put under their sleeping bags for insulation. I truly felt sorry for them. They loved the hay and they gathered up a lot of it. These were the same soldiers we got the food from for the hogs and for the people in Bend."

There was a small Italian and German prisoner of war camp within Camp Abbot. It was located on the north side of Spring River Road about half-way between the road's intersection with South Century Drive and the Harper Bridge over the Big Deschutes. Gail Baker, a man who served the U.S. Forest Service for 40 years, directed work crews from the prison camp in firefighting and routine forest labor. He is quoted in the fall 2006 issue of the *OldSmokey's Newsletter*, "The Germans were much better with tools and much easier to guard."

Grace says, "We didn't see too much of them. Dad said he really felt sorry for them as they looked so lost. I only went by there with my Dad or another adult at that time. I wasn't allowed to ride my bike or my horse outside the ranch.

"It seems that they caught a German espionage agent in Bend during the war, but it was kept very hush-hush from the public—as was the existence of a prison camp near us. The spy was taken away, but we never knew where. I don't remember when they relocated the prisoners, but it was probably after 1945 when the war in Europe ended. Everything was kept 'under wraps' at the time."

The Camp Abbot training camp only operated for 14 months before everyone left in June 1944 to go fight in Europe. Claude Junior worked in the fire department at the camp while it was operating and Dorothy, Uncle Bill's wife, also worked at the camp for a short time.

Grace reports, "My Dad worked as a civilian guard when they dismantled Camp Abbot. He was in a guard shack on the west side the railroad track. He had to stop every car and truck coming in. He was dressed in a uniform and had a lot of authority. He worked days but sometimes would work all night. When he worked nights he would drive around the perimeter of the Camp and check for anything out of place. This was when they were tearing everything down they had built for the Camp. Dad worked there for at least a year and then was able to start building up a new herd of cattle for the ranch."

The Army engineers dug a stream that came to be known as Sun River and built a northwest style officer's club made out of logs. The stream remains to this day and the building, now known as the Great Hall, serves as a meeting and conference center for Sunriver Resort.

In addition to the Great Hall, the Army left behind a road, water, and sewer system capable of supporting a small town. This was not lost on Don McCallum, a real estate attorney and president of a title company. After all the years of homesteading, buying, and selling of property in "Big Meadows," it took McCallum years to clear the titles for a contiguous 5,500 acres. McCallum then approached John Gray, the developer of Salishan, a luxurious and successful resort on the Oregon Coast. Gray presented the plans for the Sunriver Resort to the public in late April 1969 in the Great Hall.

The project took off rapidly. Within two years, the resort had plotted homesites and built the lodge, airstrip, main swimming pool, stables, bike paths, and the Meadows Golf Course. The prestigious architectural firm, Skidmore, Owings & Merrill, did some of the original site planning. Grace reports,

> "My dad was quite intrigued with the Sunriver concept when he first heard about it. People in Bend were not. They felt that the area should be left alone and not developed—because those 'California people' would come up and take over. Dad said to me one day 'I don't understand why people wouldn't want this development to come in. What in the heck could they possibly hurt in that sand and sagebrush?' He thought it was a great idea and welcomed it. He got acquainted with John Gray and they became good friends. Mr. Gray asked Dad about the history of the area and Dad gave him a lot of help. I believe it was Dad's advice that got them to save the wagon tracks of the immigrants that came through Sunriver in the 1800s.
>
> "Because of Dad's knowledge of the area, he was asked to help name the first streets in the development, near the lodge. He told me he gave the streets the names of flowers, plants, trees, Indians, and so forth. The developers wanted to recognize Dad for all his help and to acknowledge the historical role of Vandevert Ranch. They decided to name a room in the lodge the Vandevert Room. They put a nameplate on the banquet room at the north end of the lodge. My son says the Vandevert Room is where the golf trophies were kept when he played in the Oregon Pro-Am Golf Tournament in the 1980s and 90s. He loved to brag about that!
>
> "Dad was always in favor of the development and it was a blessing to Dad and my stepmother in the years after it was built. They could do their shopping only three miles from home instead of going all the way to Bend or La Pine."

CHAPTER 16

New Wife, New Home

The Forest Service made the range at Spring River available again for summer grazing after World War II and Claude Senior brought cattle back onto the ranch. On his way to the range, he passed a little store and café on the north side of Spring River Road about a mile west of the Deschutes River. Mary Jean was working at the store in the spring of 1952.

"The store was about 50 yards from the spring that was the source of Spring River," says David Vandevert. "It was where the cattle, horses, Dad, and I always drank the ice-cold water after the morning's journey from the ranch."

Evelyn Jossy, who ran the store, had a sister-in-law named Jeannie who was visiting her. The women had married the Jossy brothers, who ran the Portland-Bend trucking service. Both men had died leaving the women widows. Mary Jean mentioned to Jeannie that her dad was going to be taking cattle to the range and would stop in for pie on the way home. Jeannie thought it would be great to meet a real cowboy—arriving on his horse no less. Mary Jean introduced them that day and wrote her sister Grace in Philadelphia about the progress of the ensuing romance. "Dad and Jeannie went out to mail some letters at the mailbox. But they didn't come back right away!" Grace was very amused.

Claude Senior and Jeannie were married in Bend in October, 1952. Claude's brother Bill was the best man. A few weeks later, at least 75

Claude Senior, Jeannie Jossy Vandevert, and Dave Vandevert at the Homestead with dog Nicky.

friends arranged a chivaree. A chivaree was traditionally held the night of the wedding and involved friends banging pots and pans to make a racket outside the newlywed's house. This one was a surprise. Dave says, "My brother Claude had come to the ranch earlier in the day with Uncle Bill's pickup for a load of wood—supposedly to take to his house in Bend. But he parked it in the forest to the east of the ranch in preparation for the evening's bonfire. I knew the plans and kept quiet all day. But after sunset, here came a line of cars honking down the driveway. Dad, Jeannie and I were in the old living room of the house. When Dad heard the noise, he grabbed his shotgun and ran out the door. That scared me to death! I thought for sure he was going to shoot at the company! So I ran out and said, 'Dad, Dad. It's okay!' I didn't say anything about the ensuing party, and he just started firing the shotgun in the air—and I knew he suspected what was happening."

The couple spent their first winter in the Homestead. Jeannie loved that year—even with no running water, limited heat, and an outdoor toilet. She had lived on a ranch in Wisconsin as a child and had some idea what to expect. Grace says she always gave Jeannie a lot of credit for living in the "old" house that winter with Grace's father and brother David. But Jeannie said it was fun.

Claude and Jeannie started building a new house in early 1953 with blueprints purchased from Sears Roebuck. The lumber came from Lelco since Claude Junior had worked for the company for years and knew Leonard Lundgren, the owner, very well. The new house is a little south and east of the Homestead. Claude Senior was very involved with the construction of the new house. He was 60 years old by then and still working the ranch. He hired others to dig the basement, pour concrete, do the framing, and put in the plumbing. But he, Claude Junior, and David did the rest. The family team took the stones from the old Homestead fireplace and chimney to build the fireplace and chimney at Claude and Jeannie's new house. Claude Junior handpicked a special piece of pecked wood for the mantel. Claude Senior and Jeannie moved in before the next winter hit and were very happy with the house. It had electricity, running water, and no drafts slipping through between logs. The house was heated by forced air coming from a wood-burning furnace. The furnace was later replaced by one that used propane. Jeannie always kept the place up nicely after they built it.

The new house had four bedrooms—two up and two down—one bath, a kitchen, dining room, living room, and a very small hallway. It had an attached garage for one car. There was a large window in the living room overlooking the meadow and a great window in the kitchen to look out at the river. There was a great view from the dining room, too.

It was about that time that Mary Jean married Jack and later moved to Seattle. David was 11 in 1953 and from that time forward was the only child on the ranch. Though his Aunt Mittye, his older sisters, and

The "new" house being built in 1953 next to the log Homestead. The house was built by Claude Senior, Claude Junior, and Dave.

others had always cared for him, having Jeannie and his father married and sharing the ranch with him felt like he really had a home. He says, "I remember none of the different houses and caregivers of my early life. But I am impressed with the extended family that gave me all kinds of attention and love. I don't have any memories of moving to the ranch at that early age. It was as though I had always been there"

Dave lived on the ranch and attended the one-room schoolhouse through the spring of 1955. Dave and the new family dog, Spunky, shared a room in the basement of the new house. The basement was packed with wood in the winter and Dave got up early every morning to start the fire.

A number of movies and television shows were filmed in the area while the family lived there in the 1950s, 1960s, and 1970s. Kirk Douglas was part owner of a production company that built "Fort Benham" on a butte above Benham Falls. Logs and lumber were provided by Lelco and Brooks-Scanlon. Douglas starred in the movie "The Indian Fighter" that was shot at the fort. Six episodes of the television series, "Have Gun, Will Travel" were shot at what the series referred to as "Fort Benjamin" and at other nearby locations.

Jeannie had carried on the tradition of baking bread at the ranch. When Richard Boone, the star of "Have Gun, Will Travel" was making shows nearby, Jeannie had Boone and his wife in for fresh bread several times. They loved the bread and they probably loved visiting Claude and Jeannie as well.

Kirk Douglas once asked David to build a small hitching post in front of the Homestead. The family has wondered ever since what movie or show that hitching post appears in. But Dave got five dollars for building it!

Another star that came to the ranch was "The African Queen." Hal Bailey, one of the developers of Sunriver, bought the boat from the 1951 movie of the same name that starred Katherine Hepburn and Humphrey Bogart. The boat took people on trips up and down the Deschutes River in 1969, 1970, and 1971. It made a great chugging sound and had a loud whistle. Bailey came to Claude Senior one year to see if he could put the boat in Claude's barn over the winter. Bailey was afraid the ice would damage it. The boat came to the ranch but the door on the barn was too low. Bailey had to go elsewhere.

In the fall of 1955, Dave moved in with his brother Claude and Claude's wife Nancy on Blakely Road south of Bend so he could attend ninth grade at Bend High School. Deschutes County paid an allowance to Claude for Dave's room and board because it was easier (and probably cheaper) than arranging transportation from the ranch to Bend. During the week, Dave milked the cow for them and helped Claude Junior around his place. After ninth grade, he went to the new high school east of town and graduated in June 1960.

Dave was on the school bowling team and ran the two mile, mile, and 880 on the track team. In his junior year, one afternoon when he was bowling, his father walked into the bowling alley and told him to come outside. Dave wondered if he was in trouble. But instead, a 1952 Chevrolet two-door light green sedan was parked outside. His father said it was Dave's.

"I about fell over," says Dave. "There had been no discussion about a car. Dad said I needed it, especially on weekends to come home."

Dave went home to the ranch almost every weekend and returned on Sunday evening. Before he had his own car, his father and Jeannie usually picked him up on Fridays. Often Claude and Nancy brought him back on Sunday evenings.

If it was haying season, Dave would help his father for the entire weekend. When he was not there, however, Jeannie often drove the new John Deere tractor while Claude Senior pitched the hay. Around 1956, the family got a hay loader that fastened to the rear of the wagon and followed the rows of raked hay. It picked up the hay with forks turned by the wheels and the hay went up into the wagon on a wide conveyor belt. But the hay just went to the rear of the wagon and had to be pitched toward the front of the wagon by hand. It was quite a contraption but it worked. It made for a long string of machinery... first the tractor, then the wagon, and then the hay loader. But it was easier than pitching the hay into the wagon by hand. "We still had to pitch some hay into the wagon," says Dave, "because parts of the meadow were too small to turn the tractor, the wagon, and the hay loader.

"We had the rye baled by someone else a few years—maybe three or four. It was a big relief as pitching rye on the wagon was nasty: It was always very dusty and the rye stems were very scratchy. The meadows where we grew grass instead of rye were rough ground and sometimes too wet for the baler. So we harvested most of the grass the usual way with the hay loader." Dave helped his father cut wood on weekends and cut wood for his brother Claude at his house in Bend.

After he graduated from Bend High School, Dave attended Central Oregon Community College for two years. He worked at Wagner's grocery store in Bend, ran track for the College, and sometimes worked for Pacific Fruit Company unloading fruit and vegetables off railcars—often starting at 3:00 a.m. in the morning. He was a busy man.

In 1962, Dave went to Linfield College in McMinville, Oregon, and majored in psychology. He had a partial track scholarship and worked in the men's locker room. His Uncle Arthur sent him money for the dorm, food, and tuition. Dave says Arthur really helped a lot.

When he graduated in 1965 Dave left for Logan, Utah, for three months of Peace Corps training. Then Dave started work further from the ranch than any other family member. From 1965 to 1967, he was a Peace Corps volunteer in Shiraz, often considered the most romantic city in Iran. Shiraz is known for its poets, wine, gardens, and beautiful women. True to his ranching heritage Dave worked with 4-H Clubs and the Department of Agriculture throughout the province.

Dave stayed in Iran about two years before he returned to Fresno to work with a new Peace Corps group heading to the country. During that time, he became reacquainted with Barbara Hume whom he had met at Linfield. The two were married in the spring of 1968. They had a wedding date set earlier that year, but Dave accepted a Peace Corps training job for a group going to Afghanistan. The youthful marriage did not last long.

From 1970 to 1978 (shortly before Ayatollah Khomeini became Supreme Leader of Iran and Americans were no longer welcome), Dave shuttled between working on his Ph.D. at the University of Utah and heading the Iran-America Society and doing research at Pahlavi University in Shiraz. Dave relates how his life changed in Iran.

> "I obtained a full scholarship to the University of Tehran; but unfortunately, when I got there I had to study Persian Literature which I wasn't prepared to do. After about three months, I received a call from the Iran-America Society in Shiraz to become their director. I went there for an interview and was hired. I was very happy to be back in Shiraz again. A Canadian couple told me they wanted me to meet an Iranian woman with whom they were good friends. Shortly thereafter, I hired her as a secretary. The weeks went by, I took a trip to Tehran, and upon my return into my office pops Parichehr, closes the door, and kisses me. Was I surprised! Well, what was a man to do with such a beautiful woman? We started dating—mostly with the Canadian couple—and then she introduced me to her family."

Dave and Parichehr Dezham were married in 1972. There were many things that Parichehr had to get used to in the United States, but she generally adapted well. She liked Vandevert Ranch very much. A daughter, Tannoz (Tanny), was born to Dave and Parichehr in Salt Lake City.

Dave recalls trying to help Parichehr's brothers in 1981 at the time of the Iran/Iraq war:

> "In about 1981, the war between Iraq and Iran was in full force and Parichehr's parents were very worried about two of her brothers who would soon be eligible for the draft. Knowing it was difficult to get U.S. visas for Iranians at that time, Parichehr arranged for me to meet them in Switzerland and try to convince the American counsel to issue visas. They had Swiss visas for only about 10 days. But day after day they went to the American Consulate and were turned down. So, with only three days left on their visas, I went in with them to the counsel and said: 'I am in possession of some information that I think would be valuable to you and the U.S. State Department,' He said "Oooohhh-kay. Why don't you come in with your family tomorrow?"

"The 'information' I had was names, addresses and telephone numbers of attorneys in England, France and Spain that had inside contacts with consulates in those countries that would obtain U.S. visas for Iranians. Parichehr had given them to me at the last minute, but we did not expect to be able to use them because their fees were very high.

"So the next morning, we again went to the American Consulate. We waited all day until we were the last people and the consul called us in. I said to him, 'I have the information I promised, but I need a favor. I need all five of these people to be issued U.S. visas.' I presented the information to him, and then he went stamp, stamp, stamp...and issued their visas. Never heard from him or the State Department again! The next day, we were on a plane from Zurich to Dallas and on to L.A."

Dave and Parichehr divorced in about 1995, but Dave remains close to Parichehr and her family. Parichehr has had a successful career in engineering and has worked for Boeing in Long Beach for 23 years. She and her brothers pursue Sufism, a variety of Islam focused on the inner life. Parichehr does not pray daily, but does fast during Ramadan. Neither Dave nor Tannoz are practicing Muslims, but Dave says he now knows more about Islam than he does about Christianity.

Dave earned both a Masters and a Ph.D. in cultural anthropology from the University of Utah and another Masters in public health from UCLA. His subsequent career has centered on health education. He has written many published papers on multicultural medicine, AIDS, and healthcare in Iranian villages. Today, he is a semi-retired grant proposal writer living in Oregon City.

Grace's father, Claude Senior, continued to own the ranch until 1970, combining income from cattle, social security, and money Jeannie had from her husband's will. Then Leonard Lundgren, Claude Junior's employer at Lelco Mill and Lumber, offered to buy the ranch with a "life estate." The life estate allowed Claude Senior and Jeannie to stay on the ranch as long as they lived. Claude Senior sold the ranch on a real estate contract that gave him income every month. Grace believes Leonard took care of the taxes and even told her father he could run cattle or other stock if he wanted to. But Claude was ready to sell the cattle and did so in 1971.

Leonard Lundgren sold the ranch at a loss to two brothers from Salem who were in the business of building log homes. Then the ranch went into foreclosure and was sold in 1987 to the developers of the modern ranch, Jim and Carol Gardner. The Gardners' price in 1987 was actually lower than what Lundgren paid Claude Senior for the ranch in 1970. The Gardners eventually sold 22 lots on the ranch, each of them for more than they had paid for the entire property.

Claude Senior died in 1975, but he did get his wish to live on the ranch all his life. Grace talks about Jeannie:

> "Jeannie had no desire to leave the place even though we were all concerned about her. She said she was so happy there on the ranch that she didn't want to leave. She continued on having family reunions every year in July as she and Dad had done before. They always had them on the same weekend as the Deschutes County Historical Society (DCHS) had their Sunday picnics so that we could attend them, too. We had ours on Saturday and then went to the picnic in Bend—usually in Pioneer Park—with the DCHS people there. Dad had been their president for one year in the early 1950s. Another year Aunt Dorothy was the society's queen. The picnic was a great place to meet Dad's old friends from years back.
>
> "Now, while she lived at the ranch, Jeannie was in as good health as any lady that age could be. I was with her every summer for a week and she could carry on just fine. Jeannie was 85 when she left the ranch and, except for a fall down the basement steps one time, I believe she was always well. Her daughter Bernie came to visit a lot from Portland—as did her son Bob. Also, close friends of mine named Russell lived just a mile south of the ranch and left their horse with her. They came almost every day and to see if Jeannie was okay."

Jeannie moved from the ranch in 1989. After staying with her son in-law until 1993, she entered a foster care home where she stayed a year or so and then to another care facility closer to her son. Grace visited her in both places. She was born March 25, 1904, in Wisconsin and died in Portland on May 29, 1998. She stayed fairly well until she lost the sight in one eye. She lived to be 94.

CHAPTER 17

New Owners, New Ranch

"In 1987," says Grace, "I stopped to visit Jeannie for a couple of nights. She said she had heard that there were two buyers interested in the ranch. She thought maybe one of them might have bought it, but knew none of the details. I drove to the Sunriver Real Estate office and asked a nice young man about the Vandevert Ranch. He said, 'Gee, I'm sorry, but it is sold!' I explained that I was only looking for details and he told me that the Gardners had purchased it and that they would be coming to the ranch on Saturday."

Jim and Carol Gardner had been looking for the perfect property in Central Oregon because they loved the country and wanted to have horses. Ideally, the place would be near water and have a mountain view. The couple lived in Portland and Jim was about to leave the presidency of Lewis and Clark College. They had married after Jim graduated from Harvard and from law school at Yale. While Jim was with the Ford Foundation in Brazil, Carol started a successful business creating and marketing paper products.

Jim first saw the ranch when he went to Sunriver to visit Richard Thalheimer, a friend and the founder of Sharper Image. Back in Portland, Carol saw an ad for Vandevert Ranch in *Oregon Business*. The ad did not even mention the Little Deschutes River. When Carol called the realtor, she learned the ranch had gone through foreclosure and was owned by a bank. It was Friday and the bank was going to accept an offer on Monday.

Carol urged Jim to visit the property and he went with his friend to see it. When Jim met Jeannie, she told him about the long history of the ranch. Jim loved history and Jeannie's tales undoubtedly contributed to his instant affection for Vandevert Ranch.

"Jeannie was a pistol," says Carol. "She was a lovely woman and a real character. And she was a big thick volume of history."

Jim wanted to make an offer and Carol agreed even though she had never seen the property. "It had mountain views, a river, and plenty of room to ride horses," says Carol. The other buyers were quite angry to learn, on Monday morning, that the Gardners had trumped their bid with a full price offer.

Grace says, "I was there two weeks later when Carol visited the ranch for the first time. The Gardners brought their son Jay with them. Jim was carrying a movie camera and was taking all kinds of pictures. I simply said 'Hello' to them and pointed out a couple of places on the river that were good for swimming and where not to swim (around the big bridge—due to rocks). Jeannie seemed pleased about it all and was happy to know that someday the Gardners would be living there."

Jim and Carol's original intention was to remain the sole owners of the ranch and to live on it full time. They had no plans to develop the land and sell lots. They were excited about having their young son, Jay, eight years old in 1987, attend Sunriver Preparatory School. The Homestead was an amazing house. They could have horses and live the life they had always wanted.

Part of the deal was that Jeannie retained her right to stay on the ranch as long as she lived. The idea was that the Gardners would live in the Old Homestead once it was rebuilt and Jeannie would stay in the new house, beside the Old Homestead, that she and Claude Senior built in 1953. Grace says,

> "I think I only came down once more while Jeannie was there. She liked Jim and Carol very much. I always knew they were very caring about her. They put log siding on the house that Jeannie was living in and offered to install an automatic garage door for her. They wanted her to be comfortable. But Jeannie was bothered by all the work going

on next door at the old house. It was taking away her peace and quiet. She was getting older and her son and daughter in Portland wanted her to leave the ranch. That era had come to an end—we all loved her so much and we all were so happy that Dad had Jeannie in his life for even longer than our Mother. She left the ranch in November of 1989 and moved in with her daughter Bernie and son in-law Cecil in Portland. I think Carol wanted her to stay.

"When Jim and Carol rebuilt the Homestead, they were required to bring in a lot of dirt and make the area much higher above the river than it was in our day. It was one of the first things I noticed when I drove into the ranch and saw the restored Homestead."

The Gardners never thought they could live in the Homestead the way it was. After almost 100 years, it was a credit to Bill Vandevert that the house was standing at all. It still had no running water or central heat. But the new "Homestead" had to be built in the same location and look like the original from the outside in order to qualify as a Deschutes County Historic Resource under the county code. Jim and Carol were able to add a one-story garage tucked into the back of the house, but the biggest change was on the inside, removing part of the second floor and lifting the ceiling of the living room all the way to the roof, dominating the room with a two-story rock fireplace and chimney.

The Old Homestead from the north before it was demolished to make way for rebuilding.

Ed Adams, Central Oregon's premier log craftsman, did the log work on the kitchen. Ed says the Gardners intended to re-use all the logs from the original house and numbered each log before they removed it. Some logs were, in fact, still usable after almost 100 years.

The new 1953 house stood alone briefly before the Homestead was rebuilt. Original barn, to the left, was still standing.

But there was a problem. The contractor had not measured the house. It turned out the front part of the house was 18 feet front to back on one end and 17 feet at the other end. After he built a rectangular foundation, the logs would not fit. So the Homestead was rebuilt using all new logs.

The house used full log scribe construction with the logs spiked together as in the original. The 20 penny spikes were 10 to 12 inches long but are not visible. Ed Adams built the wall under the kitchen bay window with dovetailed corners. Ed, who has built many structures from photographs, took the design out of a book about Captain Jack, Indian leader in the Modoc Wars. The dovetails are elongated with 45° angles on the back to drain any rainwater down and away from the house. Ed built the new Homestead dock where the old wagon bridge was. He reused planks from the bridge for the deck but new logs for the supporting structure.

The Homestead being rebuilt in 1988.

Jim and Carol decorated the Homestead interior with exquisite Indian and western artifacts. The house was featured in the June 1998 issue of *Architectural Digest*.

The new Homestead seen from the riverbank.

From then on, Ed Adams and Jim Gardner collaborated on the design of many log structures around the ranch. They designed the bridge rails, the mailboxes, and the road signs from photos they saw in a book about national park construction. The picnic tables were copies of old ones at the nearby Lava Cast Forest. The tables were falling apart. A week after Ed sketched and measured them, the Forest Service took them away.

Ed Adams at a ranch picnic table he modeled after those found at the Lava Cast Forest.

Ed helped Jim with the design of the barn, but Bill Betzer, a friend of Ed's, built the barn because Ed was so busy. Ed built the maintenance shed. The barn and the maintenance building both used post and beam construction that incorporated logs, rather than traditional log construction. The vertical posts were full logs with knee braces. The upstairs room at the barn used relatively unusual jowled posts because Jim did not want to detract from the open space by using angle braces. The jowled posts required starting with 12 x 16 inch posts and narrowing them everywhere except at the top.

A jowled post, used to provide a more open space in the common room above the stables.

Jim and Carol also renovated the schoolhouse, originally built in 1925. They moved the windows from the east side to the west side, installed electric heat and a bathroom, and painted the exterior green to better fit into the woodland setting. Where wood needed to be replaced, they were scrupulous in replacing it with

The Harper School today. The windows were moved to the west side and the building was painted green to blend with the trees.

exact replicas, down to having knives tooled to manufacture bead board designs that had been discontinued decades earlier. They bought old desks along with books and teaching materials from the 1930s, 1940s, and 1950s.

Today the classroom looks very much the way it did when the Vandevert children went to school there. Ranch owners use it for small meetings and social events. On "Pioneer Day," the ranch hosts a visit from local schoolchildren who come dressed like students 100 years earlier, learning what school was like long before their time.

Carol cannot remember when she and Jim decided to develop Vandevert and sell lots. But she remembers how. When friends came to visit the Gardners, they all wanted to live there as well. Indeed, several of the original buyers were already friends of the Gardners, one of them going all the way back to the Harvard football team.

The Gardners had an opportunity to acquire an additional 80 acres from the Forest Service and they took it. It was woodland that abutted the south half of the ranch on the west side. There was nothing on it but the remains of the cabin Uncle Bill had started to build many years earlier. The Gardners actually acquired other land contiguous to the Deschutes National Forest and swapped it with the Forest Service for the 80 acres contiguous to the ranch.

Carol's parents had just come to visit the Gardners at the ranch when, one day, Carol looked out of Jay's window to see flames shooting up from the new woodlands to the west. It was a terrifying sight. Carol's first reaction was that it could not possibly be happening. Then she blinked and realized it was for real. She was on the phone immediately and the response was rapid.

Les Joslin says he fought that fire with the Sunriver Fire Department, primarily patrolling the east side of the river putting out spot fires. The fire was out by the end of the day. It never came close to the Homestead. The fire had escaped from a purposely lit refuse fire just west of the ranch and burned about 37 acres. Aside from the immediate fear it induced, the fire turned out to be a good thing. Logging had left the area full of small trees and logs not worth hauling away. After the fire, the area provided a clear view of Mt. Bachelor from the future barn and became a spacious horse pasture.

The development of the ranch was Jim and Carol's team effort. They shared in the creation of the plan and in the marketing of the properties. In February of 1992, almost exactly 100 years after the Vandevert family moved to the ranch, Jim and Carol filed Articles of Incorporation for the new Vandevert Ranch.

The development plan called for 22 lots, including one that encompassed the rebuilt Homestead and the 1953 house, now called the Guest House. There would be 15 lots on the east side of the ranch overlooking the meadow. In Phase 2, seven lots would overlook the river from the west side. Two roads, Schoolhouse and Hashknife, would form a horseshoe open to the north with a new bridge where the horseshoe crossed the river south of the Homestead. Each lot on the east side had its own well and sewer system, while the lots on the west were connected to water and sewer extended from the Crosswater systems to the north.

The Gardners hired Vic Russell to dig a pond in front of five lots on the east side of the ranch. Rainbow Lake, as they decided to call it, enhanced the view toward Mt. Bachelor and provided all the new owners with trout fishing. The Gardners used the spoils from the excavation to build a high berm between the ranch and South Century Drive. The berm cut road noise, provided privacy, and also prevented headlights on Schoolhouse Road from confusing drivers on South Century.

At Ed Adam's suggestion, Jim logged the roads with horses to minimize damage to the ground and surrounding vegetation. The man who did the work lived on site in a tent. The horses, named Nip and Tuck, were "Fjords," similar to Clydesdales but smaller.

The most critical construction project was the bridge over the Little Deschutes. It gave access to the Phase 2 lots, the barn, corrals, kennel, ranch office, and the maintenance building—all west of the river. The Hashknife bridge was designed so any floods would go to either side rather than pushing against the bridge. The approaches might have to be rebuilt after a big flood but the bridge would stand. No floods have threatened the bridge or its approaches since it was built.

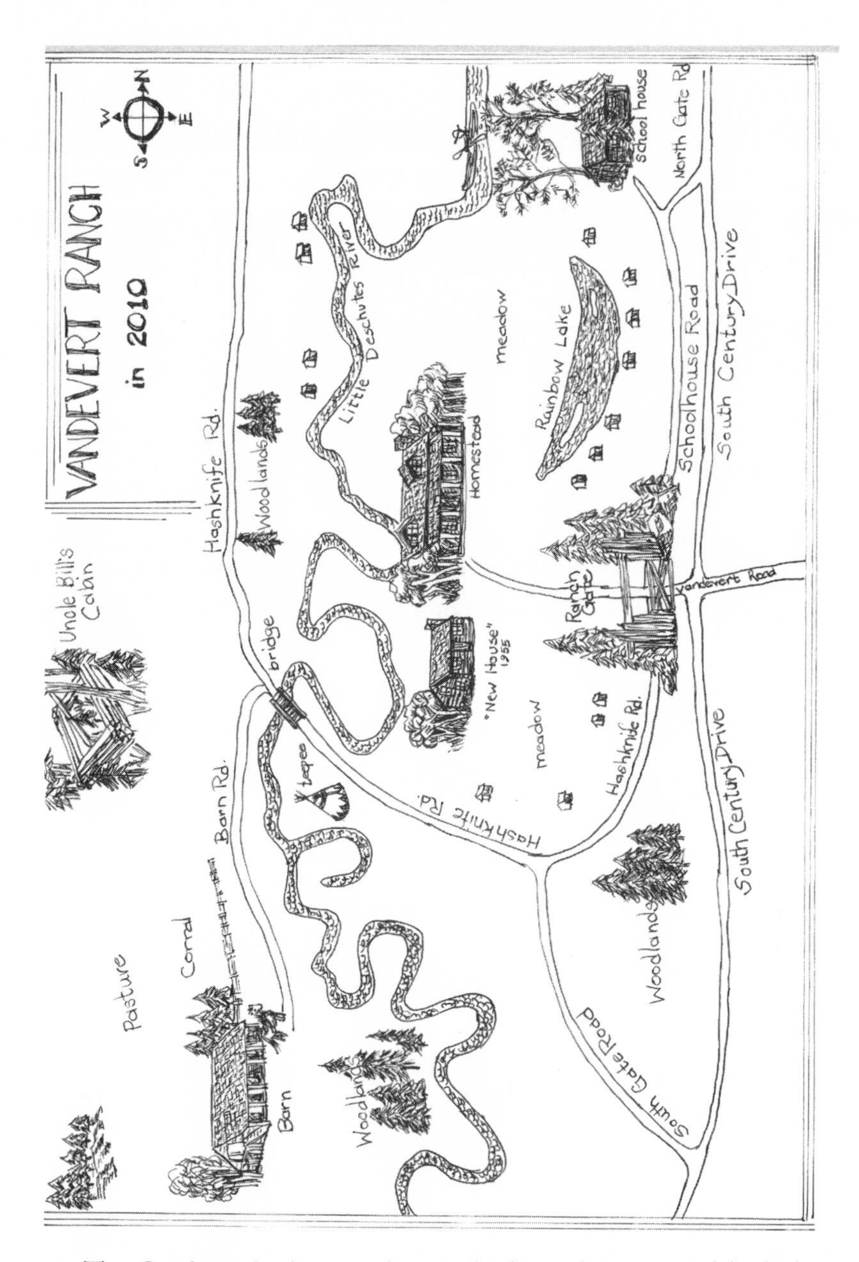

The Gardners built a gazebo overlooking the river and had plans to build a tennis court. But the early lot owners said they would rather have the money for the tennis court transferred to the new homeowners association. The Gardners did construct a teepee on a platform in a small clearing east of the river and it has remained one of the delights of the ranch.

The development was successful from the very beginning to the sale of the last lot. Jim and Carol's desire to share their dream kindled the same love of the ranch in others. The momentum kept picking up. They were never worried that it would not be successful.

About a third of the new owners came from Portland or Salem, a third from Northern California, and a third from Southern California. Over half of the buyers already owned a home in Central Oregon or had strong ties to the area. In a 2010 survey asking owners the reasons they chose Vandevert Ranch, 100% agreed it was the opportunity to own a 400-acre ranch while sharing the cost and not having to manage it day to day. Other significant reasons were the beauty of the land and the privacy of a gated community with no resort or other outside traffic.

In the meantime, Bend was growing rapidly. Retirees and young people were attracted by the "wild and sublime" scenery, the sunny weather, the opportunities for outdoor recreation, and the low cost of living. The city's population grew 154% from 1990 to 2000 and another 58% by 2009. Even the old mills took on a new life when a developer named Bill Smith bought them in 1993 and turned the land into single-family homes, townhomes, shops, restaurants, a theater, and offices. Three of the tall Brooks-Scanlon smoke stacks, now brightly painted with an American flag on top, mark the site of the new "Old Mill District." Across the river, on the site of the Shevlin-Hixon mill, a park-like amphitheater that can accommodate 8,000 people has seen performances by Willie Nelson, Bob Dylan, B.B. King, Bonnie Raitt, and other well-known artists.

Carol Gardner imagined she would be living in the Homestead for the rest of her life, surrounded by people she knew and loved. It was her dream. Carol thought the dream would go on forever but, unfortunately, Jim decided to leave the marriage. Carol thinks and hopes the ranch has fulfilled the dreams of others. She says she may still wind up there.

Carol Gardner (on right) with the authors.

Carol moved to Portland and changed her disadvantage into an advantage. Using her background as a creative director in advertising, Carol turned her English bulldog, Zelda, into an international icon who now appears on greeting cards, calendars, books, and many other items. Hallmark bought into "Zelda Wisdom" and made it their number one mass market greeting card. Zelda's legacy will be long-lasting. A larger-than-life statue now greets guests at the Heathman Hotel in Portland.

Carol says, "Zelda and I started out as underdogs, but we are proof that you don't have to be thin, rich, young or wrinkle-free to be successful."

Jim went on to develop The Ranch at the Canyons in Terrebonne, Oregon, with a Tuscan and Napa Valley wine-growing theme. As of this writing, the Gardner's son, Jay, just received his Ph.D. from the medical school at the University of California in San Francisco and will soon receive his MD from UCSF as well.

The Gardners turned the ranch over to the homeowners association, called The Vandevert Ranch Association, on July 5, 1996. At that time, they had sold 15 of the 22 lots. Houses were completed, or near completion, on four lots and construction was underway on three more. There are now 17 houses on the ranch—including the Homestead and the "new" house built by Claude Vandevert Senior in 1953.

CHAPTER 18

New Log Houses

The beauty of log houses comes first from the logs themselves - wood in close to its natural state. Log construction displays the builder's skill in fitting the logs together. Snug cabins remind us of our ancestors taming the wilderness with the materials they had at hand. Grand lodges bring dreams of leisurely days away from the cares of civilization, of fishing in the summer, hunting in the fall, and skiing in the winter. People who know log houses say Vandevert Ranch has the greatest concentration of log homes in the West. Yet the Vandevert houses vary widely in their construction and in the inspirations for their designs.

A log house that is built to last must use special techniques to address three issues unique to log construction—settling, limitations on long spans, and an inherent (but surmountable) vulnerability to rain and snow.

Logs are thicker than lumber and it takes longer for the logs to lose their natural moisture. Logs continue to lose water and shrink after the house is built. The house "settles." If the logs fit together well ("scribed" so the bottom of one horizontal log fits the top of the log below it), this settling is not a problem for the logs themselves—though the caulk or "chinking" between the logs will need periodic repair. But the doors and windows do not settle along with the logs. They need hidden spaces in the walls that they can move into as the logs settle around them (mostly spaces inside the log above the window or door).

These "slip joints" are used in seven of the nine "full log" houses on the ranch. "Full log" construction is what people usually imagine when they think of log houses. Full log uses completely round logs, laid on top of one another to make the walls and hold up the roof. The logs are visible on both the inside and outside of the wall.

The eighth full log house on the ranch, on the lot called "Broken Top" after a mountain in the Cascades, is "pinned" to make it a "non-settling" full log house. The pins are steel rods running vertically through the logs and attaching to steel plates between the logs. The weight of the roof is resting on the steel rods, not on the logs. Each of the logs is resting on the steel plates beneath it. Though the logs shrink, the house does not settle.

The ninth full log house, "Riverpoint," uses a different approach. It is the only house on the ranch to use "post and beam" construction to support the roof. The weight of the roof is born by vertical log posts with beams running across the top of them. Where there are full log walls they fit between the posts and help support the roof. Screw jacks under the vertical posts allow the posts to be lowered when the logs settle so gaps do not open up between the tops of the log walls and the

Post and beam construction with full log walls and extensive window openings at Riverpoint.

beams above them that rest on the posts. In the other full log houses on the ranch, wherever there is a vertical support that does not settle, there are screw jacks underneath it so the support can be adjusted.

Six houses on the ranch side-step the settling issue by using "half-log" construction instead of full log. These houses are framed with lumber and sheeted with plywood, much like a conventional house. The builder cuts logs in half lengthwise and bolts the halves to the plywood and frame. He leaves the ends of some logs round and crosses the log ends at the corners so the house still looks like a full log house from the outside. The inside walls are flat like those in a frame house. The half-logs still shrink and require re-chinking, but the roof rests on the frame and the house does not settle. The only way to tell a good half-log house from a full log house from the outside is to look at the spaces between the logs, particularly at the corners after the house has been up for a few years. If the logs are pressed tight together then the house is full log. The logs have settled down on each other. If there are small gaps between the logs then the frame is holding each log in place and the house is half-log construction.

Full log corners on a half-log wall.

When owners want large openings for windows, logs are often not strong enough to support the wall and roof above the window without sagging or twisting over time. Some of the houses on the ranch use hidden steel "moment frames" to provide the necessary strength. "Stagecoach" uses steel hidden inside a 43-foot-long log to span a very large upstairs room.

A steel moment frame may be used to strengthen a large opening in a log house.

The windows built around the moment frame shown above.

Weather can be particularly hard on full log and half-log houses because the logs act like shelves—holding rainwater and snow longer than straight vertical walls. All logs need to be rotated so the biggest "check" (a wedge-shaped crack running lengthwise) faces down. Checks open up as the log dries and every log has at least one of them. All checks need to be caulked. The best defense on a full log or half-log house is regular treatment with preservatives and protective coatings. Fortunately, this is less expensive than paint.

But two of the houses on the ranch, "Arrowhead" and "Indian Meadow" have significantly reduced the weathering problem by using "hewn log siding" instead of full log or half-log construction. The round part of the log is cut off with an adze, a kind of axe with the blade turned 90°, so the outside wall is flat. The chinking is flush with the outside of the logs. Water runs straight down the outside of the exterior wall.

Hewn log siding.

Ed Adams was the log subcontractor on eight of the houses at the ranch. Ed's road to becoming the premier log craftsman in Central Oregon is an interesting one. He was home on leave from the Army in 1972 and went to see his old football coach who was tending bar. He ran into a friend who wanted to go into the business of building log hunting cabins and recruited Ed to join him. Back in the Army in Europe, Ed read all he could about log construction and, at some risk to his health, sought out old log farmhouses in the Bavarian countryside. He did not speak German and some of the farmers did not appreciate his poking around their houses.

In 1974, Ed's friend was killed in an accident, but Ed's plans had already grown from simple hunting cabins to larger log houses. For one thing, he wanted to build his own log home. Ed had some prior construction experience but not with logs. He knew he would have to learn from someone and approached Oregon Log Homes. He told them he would work for free until they thought he was worth paying. It took only three days.

Oregon Log Homes, and most other log builders, actually built the homes in their own yards, disassembled them, and shipped a carefully numbered "log package" to the building site. The company had six "set-up" men who worked in the yard and were in charge of selecting logs and placing them in the house. Set-up required skill and an eye for situating the logs so they did not look squashed. Ed worked for each of the set-up men and learned from all of them. After six months, he became a set-up man himself, specializing in full scribe houses. As this book goes to press, Ed is building his second log house for himself.

All the full log houses that Ed built on the ranch, except for "Heritage," are "full scribe," an exacting technique not often used in this country. Not only are the logs shaped to fit the idiosyncrasies of the logs above and below them, but there is a notch cut on the bottom of each log that runs the length of the log. There is a corresponding flange or "steeple" on the top of the log below it so the logs fit together tightly. To hold the logs down in case of an earthquake, Ed drilled holes down through the logs and inserted threaded steel rods that were connected to the roof and the foundation. There were rods on either side of each door or window and four rods near each corner. Unlike a "pinned" log house, these rods were to hold the wall together, not to support the logs or the roof. For lateral stability in the walls, Ed inserted maple dowels into adjacent logs at intervals of two feet or less. The 18-inch long dowels, 1 1/8 inch in diameter, were waxed and fitted into holes of the same diameter but deeper. The dowels drove themselves further into the logs as the logs settled.

Janet Jarvis of Sun Valley, Idaho, designed eight of the houses on the ranch. She almost turned down the first request. She had designed two log homes in the San Juan Islands and others in Ketchum, Idaho, and Jackson Hole. She was reluctant to be pigeonholed as "The Log Lady." But Janet had gone to the University of Oregon and spent time in Bend. Once she saw the river and mountains at Vandevert Ranch, she was committed. She has since escaped the "Log Lady" nickname and designs homes throughout the West in a variety of styles.

"What struck me first about the ranch," says Janet, "was the sense of permanence. I enjoyed the history about the people who had lived there. When the developer wanted log construction he set a tone that would carry through." Other architects came to the ranch from Bend, Portland, Seattle, Bozeman, and even Minneapolis.

"I wouldn't characterize my log houses as Northwestern or even Western," says Janet. "They go back to the roots of sophisticated log construction in Scandinavia, Finland, and Russia." (Some Russian churches built in the 1600s were more than 150 log courses high.)

Contrary to the popular image, the Jamestown settlers and the Pilgrims in Massachusetts did not live in log cabins. They did not know how to build them. It was not until Swedes and Finns arrived later in the 1600s that Americans started building with logs. As the frontier moved west, the log cabin became the dominant form of shelter for pioneers. A chief advantage of a log cabin was that it could be built quickly. When settlers had more time, especially east of the Mississippi, they gravitated to hewn logs because they would last longer and the flat walls looked more civilized. By the time western settlers started to value comfort over speed, milled lumber was generally available and they stopped building log cabins altogether. In 1892, of course, Bill Vandevert was still too far from a mill to pay for bringing in lumber. He used the trees that grew up around him.

Vandevert Ranch Log House Architects and Builders

Lot Name	Architect	Contractor	Log Type
The Antlers	Janet Jarvis, The Jarvis Group	Sun Forest	Half-Log
Arrowhead	Thomas Thompson	Aware Construction	Hewn Siding
Big Sky	Kent Duffy, SRG Partnership	BJ Davis Construction	Full Log
Broken Top	Neal Huston	Oregon Log Homes	Pinned[1]
Crooked Tree	Janet Jarvis, The Jarvis Group	Sun Forest	Half-Log
Four Peaks	Janet Jarvis, The Jarvis Group	Sun Forest	Half-Log
Heritage	David Leavingood	Sun Forest	Full Log
Homestead	W.P. Vandevert	Oregon Log Homes[2]	Full
Homestead Guest House	Sears Roebuck	Claude Vandevert Senior	Half-Log[3]
Indian Meadows	Janet Jarvis, The Jarvis Group	Sun Forest/S. Bennett	Hewn Siding
Little River	Jerry Locati, Locati Architects	Steve Bennett & Company	Half-Log
Osprey	Janet Jarvis, The Jarvis Group	Mutchler Construction	Full Log
Otter Point	Janet Jarvis, The Jarvis Group	Sun Forest	Full Log
Oxbow	Janet Jarvis, The Jarvis Group	Mutchler Construction	Full Log & Half-Log
Ponderosa	Janet Jarvis, The Jarvis Group	Sun Forest	Full Log[4]
Riverpoint	Jean Larsen, Rehkamp Larsen	Sun Forest	Full Log
Stagecoach	Steve Van Sant	Ross Alexander	Full Log

[1] Non-settling full log, saddle notched, steel pins with steel plates between logs.
[2] Ed Adams built new Homestead kitchen, trusses, and roof.
[3] The New House/Guest House log siding was added in about 1990.
[4] In addition to regular chinking, Ponderosa is chinked on the inside with scribed saplings between the logs.

Arthur and Cindy Thiede report in *American Log Homes* "...around the turn of the 20th century, log building enjoyed a glorified resurgence." It was in the Great Camps of the Adirondacks built as summer retreats by the wealthiest families in New York. On Vandevert Ranch, "Osprey" is the house that adheres most closely to the Great Camp ideal. Adirondack elements appearing in the house are extensive log porch railings, diamond paned windows, and a stone foundation inset with low arched iron grates.

Log architecture was one of the few beneficiaries of the Great Depression in the 1930s. The federal government hired the unemployed to build lookout towers, ranger stations, lodges, and bridges for the Forest Service and the National Park Service. "Heritage," built with large full logs, river rock, and a unique octagonal lookout tower, is the house on the ranch that most faithfully approaches the National Park ideal. The logs are the largest on the ranch and Heritage is the only full log house that relies entirely on chinking between the logs without scribing a notch into the upper log and a steeple into the log below it.

The octagonal watchtower at Heritage is modeled on National Park architecture.

Janet Jarvis reports, "For a long time, log houses followed the plans provided by log home companies. The plans were not specific for each client. It was only in the 1980s that people started going to architects."

"Every site in Vandevert is completely different and every house is unique," says Janet. "I spent a lot of time on each site I worked on—taking photos, doing solar studies, and checking the view from each room. The outside rooms, like decks, porches, and patios, are as important as the inside rooms."

One of the first houses built on the ranch was Pete and Nancy Newell's full log house "Ponderosa," overlooking Rainbow Lake. Pete had multiple sets of Lincoln Logs as a boy and always imagined building a real log house. He learned in studying modern log construction that log houses could be made water tight, air tight, and able to deal with settling. It was possible to build a log house to modern standards without compromising livability. But Pete and Nancy felt strongly they wanted an architect who had log experience because log construction had so many singular aspects to it. They discovered that Janet Jarvis had designed a log house in Ketchum, Idaho, for Nancy's sister's husband.

The Newells did not model their house on any others. They told Janet what they wanted for space, with a lengthy list of needs and wants, and Janet created the overall design. But the Newells did a lot of research and Pete nitpicked the plans with Janet all the time. They wanted every room to look at the view, leading to a long narrow house. Pete and Nancy were delighted with the result. But over time, they came to want a larger master closet. They went back to Janet and this time decided to use log siding to extend the end of the house. The logs came for free because "Osprey" was being built at that time and had extra logs.

It was Pete Newell who encouraged the Gardners to make the log construction requirements even stronger than in the original owner's agreement. Pete felt that good guidelines would make the ranch a distinctive community that the owners could be proud of. The design review guidelines were subsequently tightened up. Pete says he has looked at a lot of log homes and believes the vast majority of homes on the ranch turned out to be excellent. He does not know of any other community like it in the country.

The Adirondack Great Camp inspired Osprey with its unusual eyebrow window.

Pete, who was active on the Design Review Committee for years, felt that being dictatorial about specific designs would take the fun out of building for the owners. In another community where the Newells attempted to build a house, they found the stringent rules made the houses look too similar. Pete says his Design Review Committee never made any attempt to influence aesthetics.

Two of the houses, "Big Sky" and "Osprey," have eyebrow windows—relatively unusual in log houses. Also unusual are the massive stone entrance at "Oxbow" and the curved hallway and deck at "Little

The Ed Adams on the curved deck he built with a curved roof.
Ed's half-log wall with full log corner behind him.

River." "Stagecoach," "Big Sky" and "Osprey" are full log houses that feature "Swedish Cope." Where the logs meet at the corners, there is an arc cut into the bottom of each log that fits the top of the log below it.

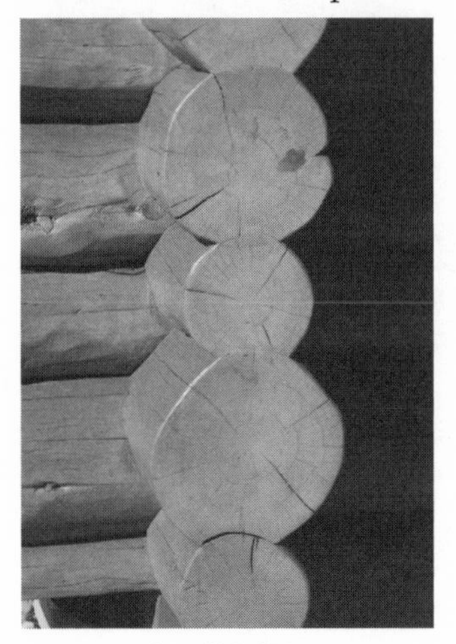

Swedish Cope.

As an example of design flexibility, "Riverpoint" is the most unique house on the ranch. Tim and Rene Finnegan, from Minnesota and North Dakota, had always imagined a house in the Prairie Style pioneered by Frank Lloyd Wright. Their architect, Jean Larson of Rehkamp Larson in Minneapolis, integrated some of the principles of Prairie Style into what is very much a traditional full log house. "The guiding principles of the Prairie Style are a close relationship to nature and the idea of 'breaking the box' between the interior and exterior," says Jean. "There is an interesting play in Riverpoint between the solid log walls and the horizontal ribbons of glass that bring the outside in. The house is hinged in the middle so, as you follow the stone entry walk, continuing like a river through the front door, you have a view across the house to the Little Deschutes itself. The house comes up out of the site with a stone wall that rises to the building and a supporting post by the front door made from a tree trunk. The roots reach down to the ground."

The house incorporates the open floor plan, central chimney, and horizontal rows of windows that are formal elements of the Prairie Style. Indeed, the log walls and log trellis over the deck extend the Wright emphasis on horizontal lines. The house mixes styles, including a touch of Modernism in the blue window trim. But the authentic full log construction requires a very well thought-out use of space. "I don't know of any other house quite like it," says Jean, "in Oregon, Minnesota, or anywhere else."

Grace says she likes all the new houses. "I've always thought the Gardners did a great job in developing the whole thing—the setting of the homes with trees around and yet with views—and leaving the meadows alone. When someone asks me about the new homes on the ranch and what they are like, I go into a stream of ecstasy over them! I tell the people where they are located and about the people that live there. I drag pictures out to show them!

"Some of my cousins thought that selling the ranch was a very bad idea and they wanted nothing to do with the place after the Gardners bought it. But I think it has turned out better than I could have ever imagined. I am so happy that people are living there and enjoying it so much."

Bibliography

Alt, David D. and Hyndman, Donald W. *Roadside Geology of Oregon.* Missoula MT: Mountain Press Publishing Company, 1978.

Baehr, Russell. *Oregon's Outback, Tales and Legends from Beyond the High Cascades.* Bend, OR: Maverick Publications, 1988.

Bill Vandevert, Bear Hunter, Bend Oregon. *The Oregon Journal.* November 22–23, 1922.

Brogan, Phil F. *East of the Cascades.* Portland, OR: Binford & Mort, 1964. Third Edition 1971.

Carlock, Robert H. *The Hashknife, The Early Days of the Aztec Land and Cattle Company Limited.* Tucson, AZ: Westernlore Press, 1994.

Celebration is Big Success. *La Pine Intermountain,* July 7, 1921.

Central Oregon Fact Book. Bend, OR: Economic Development for Central Oregon, Inc., 2004.

Coe, Urling C. *Frontier Doctor, Observations on Central Oregon and the Changing West.* Corvallis, OR: Oregon State University Press, 1996. Originally published: Macmillan Co., 1940.

Connolly, Thomas J. *Newberry Crater, A Ten-Thousand-Year Record of Human Occupation and Environmental Change in the Basin-Plateau Borderlands.* Salt Lake City, UT: University of Utah Press, 1999.

Crowell, James L. *Frontier Publisher.* Bend, OR: Deschutes County Historical Society, 2008.

Deschutes County Historical Society. *Images of America Bend.* San Francisco, CA: Arcadia Publishing, 2009.

Friends of the La Pine Library. *History of the La Pine Pioneers*, Bend, OR: Maverick Publications, 2000.

From Cheney, Washington, to Watsonville, California 1898. Mother's Diary, with commentary by John Francis Lemon some 50 years later.

Furry, Darrin. *Beyond Sagebrush—Secrets of Central Oregon's Natural World.* Bend, OR: DF Publications 2008.

Gardner, Jim. W.P. Vandevert: The great adventurer finally settles on the Little Deschutes. *Sunriver Sun*, n.d.

Good, Albert H. *Park and Recreation Structures*. New York, NY: Princeton Architectural Press, Inc., 1999 (Originally published in 1938 by the U.S. Dept. of the Interior and National Parks Service).

Gregory, Ronald L. *Life in Railroad Logging Camps of the Shevlin-Hixon Company, 1916–1950*. Corvallis, OR: Oregon State University, 2001.

Hatton, Raymond R. *High Country of Central Oregon.* Portland, OR: Binford & Mort, 1980.

Hatton, Raymond R. *High Desert of Central Oregon.* Portland, OR: Binford & Mort, 1977. Third edition 1997.

Historic Vandevert Collection to Find Home at Museum. *High Desert Quarterly*, June 1998.

Hughes, Stella. *Hashknife Cowboy, Recollections of Mack Hughes*. Tucson, AZ: The University of Arizona Press, 1984

Jensen, Robert A. *Roadside Guide to the Geology of Newberry Volcano, Third Edition*. Bend, OR: CenOreGeoPub, 2000

Jones, Randall S. Bend Resident Relates Stirring Story of Indian Raid on Pioneer Travelers, *Oregon Historical Society*. SB#272

Little Known Tales from Oregon History, Volumes I-IV. Bend, OR: Sun Publishing, 1988

Lowry, Nita. *The Triangle Outfit: The true story of one man's dream and the many people who helped make it a reality in central Oregon country*. Jordan Valley, OR: Nita Lowry, 1995

Mass, Cliff. *The Weather of the Pacific Northwest*. Seattle, WA: University of Washington Press, 2008.

McNellis, Grace Vandevert. *Home on the Vandevert Ranch.* Gig Harbor, WA: Red Apple Publishing, 1999.

Nielsen, Lawrence E., Newman, Doug, and McCart, George. *Pioneer Roads in Central Oregon*. Bend, OR: Maverick Publications, 1985.

Pizzi, Donna. An Oregon Pioneer, Restoring the Spirit of A Historic Log Cabin. *Architectural Digest*. June 1998, p. 228-233, 254.

Power, Evada R. Old Days Revived in Stories Told by William Vandevert, of La Pine. *The Redmond Spokesman*, August 20, 1936

Quinn, James W. and Redding, Paul. *Sunriver, The First 20 Years*. Self-published 1990.

Ramsey, Jarold. *New Era, Reflections on the Human and Natural History of Central Oregon*. Corvallis, OR: Oregon State University Press, 2003.

Ridgley, Veerland A. *History and Homesteaders of the La Pine Country*. Bend, OR: Maverick Publications 1993

Riis, John. *Ranger Trails*. Richmond, VA: The Dietz Press, 1937. Reprinted with a prologue and extensive epilogue by Martha Riis Moore and Les Joslin in 2008 as *Ranger Trails: The Life and Times of a Pioneer U.S. Forest Service Ranger in the West on the La Sal, Santa Barbara, Cache, and Deschutes National Forests, 1907-1913*. Bend, OR, Wilderness Associates.

Stranahan, Martha. A Pioneering Family. *Ruralite*, August 1977

Strope, Nancy. *History of Vandevert's*, monograph written in Redmond, Oregon, 1970.

Taylor, George H. and Hannan, Chris. *The Climate of Oregon*. Corvallis, OR: Oregon State University Press, 1999.

Thiede, Arthur and Teipner, Cindy. *American Log Homes*. Layton, UT: Gibbs Smith, 1986.

Tupper, Melany. *High Desert Roses, Volume 1, Significant Stories from Central Oregon*. 1st Books Library, 2003.

Vandevert, Claude Senior. *Indian Meadows*, unpublished transcript of monologue, 1971

Vaughn, Thomas, ed. *High and Mighty, Select Sketches about the Deschutes Country*. Portland, OR: Oregon Historical Society, 1981.

Williams, Elsie Horn. *A Pictorial History of the Bend Country*. Virginia Beach, VA: The Donning Company, 1983.

Additional photographs, articles, letters, and memoirs are available on the Vandevert Ranch website—www.vandevertranch.org

Index

D

G

H

I

J

K

L

N

O

Q

R

T

U

V

W

Y

Z

Vandevert

The Hundred Year History of a Central Oregon Ranch

Order Form for Autographed Copies

Readers may order copies autographed by both authors by sending a check or money order for $19.95 US ($16.95 book price + $3.00 for shipping and handling) to:

Grace V. McNellis
P.O. Box 1524
Gig Harbor, WA 98335-3524
Phone (253)858-7420

State of Washington residents please add 8% sales tax ($1.36). Sorry – credit cards and purchase orders not accepted.

Please specify:
Autographed to (e.g. "To Bill and Sadie")

____

Message with autograph (check one or write custom message).

___ (No Message)

___ Best wishes

___ Enjoy the book!

___ Custom message (maximum 20 words) ______________________________

____

____

Shipping Address:

Name____

Address1 ____

Address2 ____

City ____

State/Province ______________ Zip/Postal Code ________________

E-mail (will not be sold or shared) _____________________________

Grace Vandevert McNellis' earlier book, *Home on the Vandevert Ranch,* is out of print. Fortunately, high quality CD's of Grace reading *Home* in her own delightful voice are still available. For this unique record of life on the Vandevert Ranch, send a check for $12.95 made out to Grace McNellis to:

Vandevert CD
c/o Ms. Grace McNellis
P.O. Box 1524
Gig Harbor
Washington 98335-3524

The $12.95 includes the CD as well as shipping and handling within the United States. Be sure to include your shipping address (with your telephone number and E-mail address to help assure accurate delivery). State of Washington residents please add $.80 for state sales tax.